Vunzi

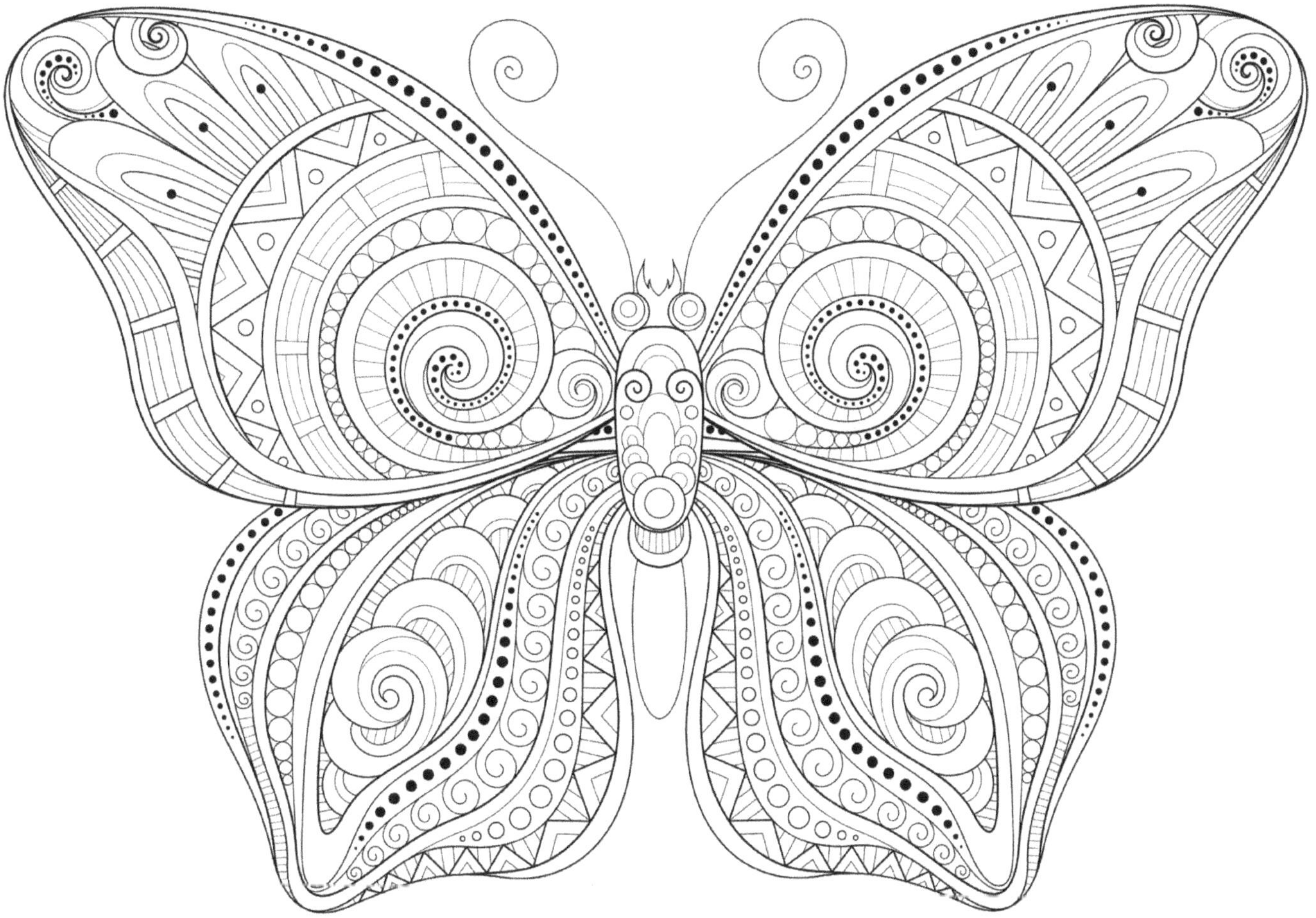

ANIMALS

Coloring Book For Adults

ISBN-13: 978-1-0723-6257-9

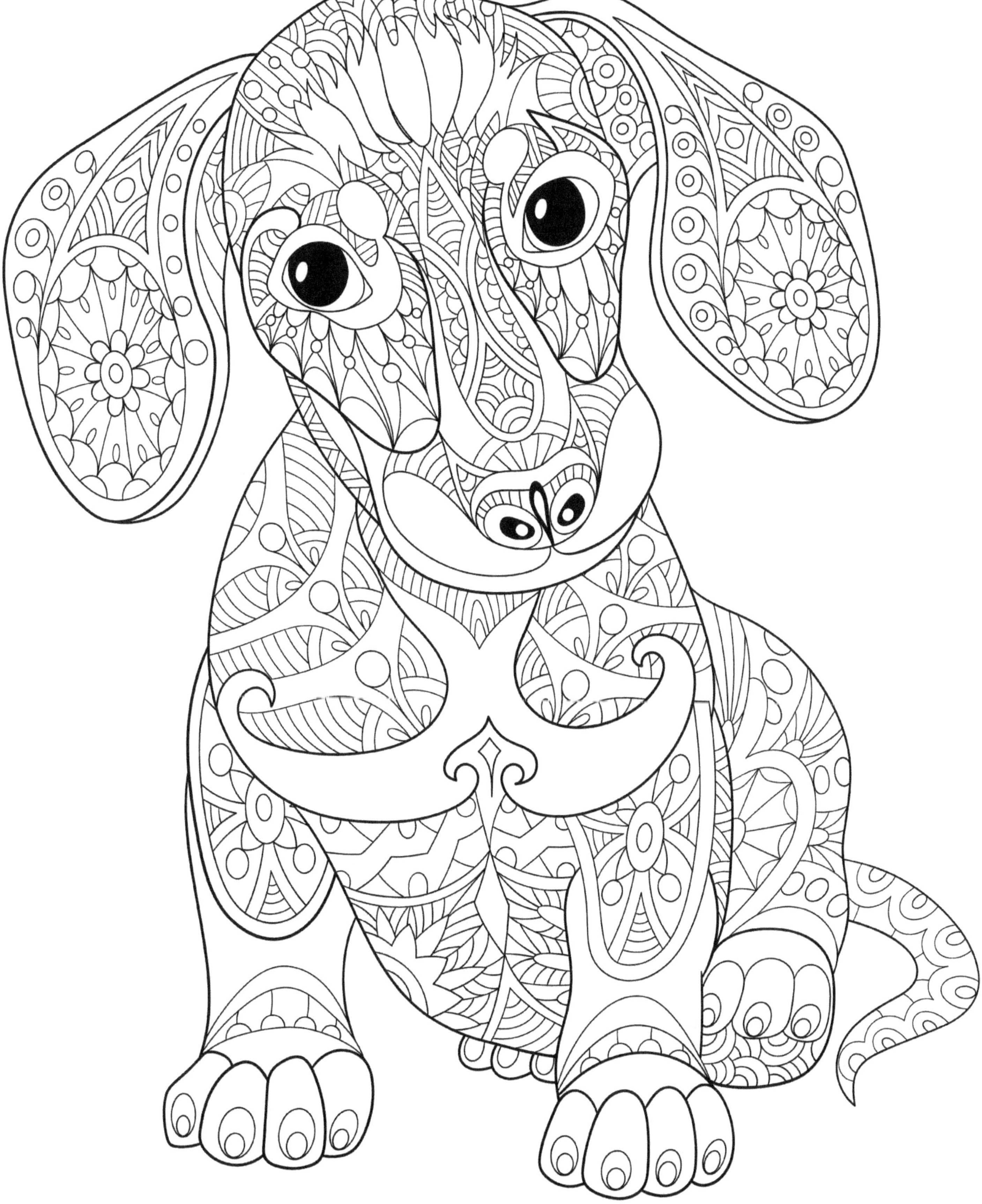

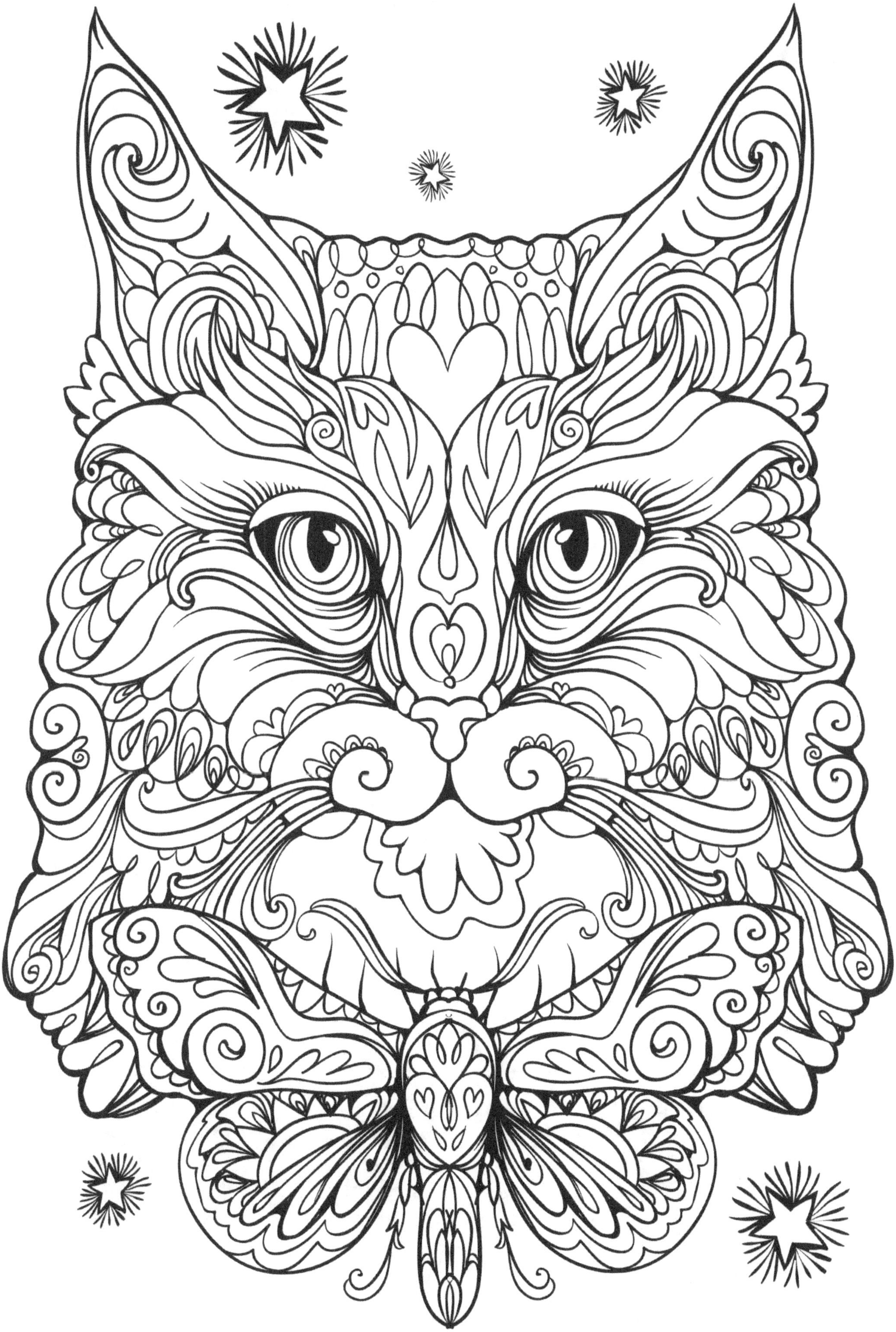

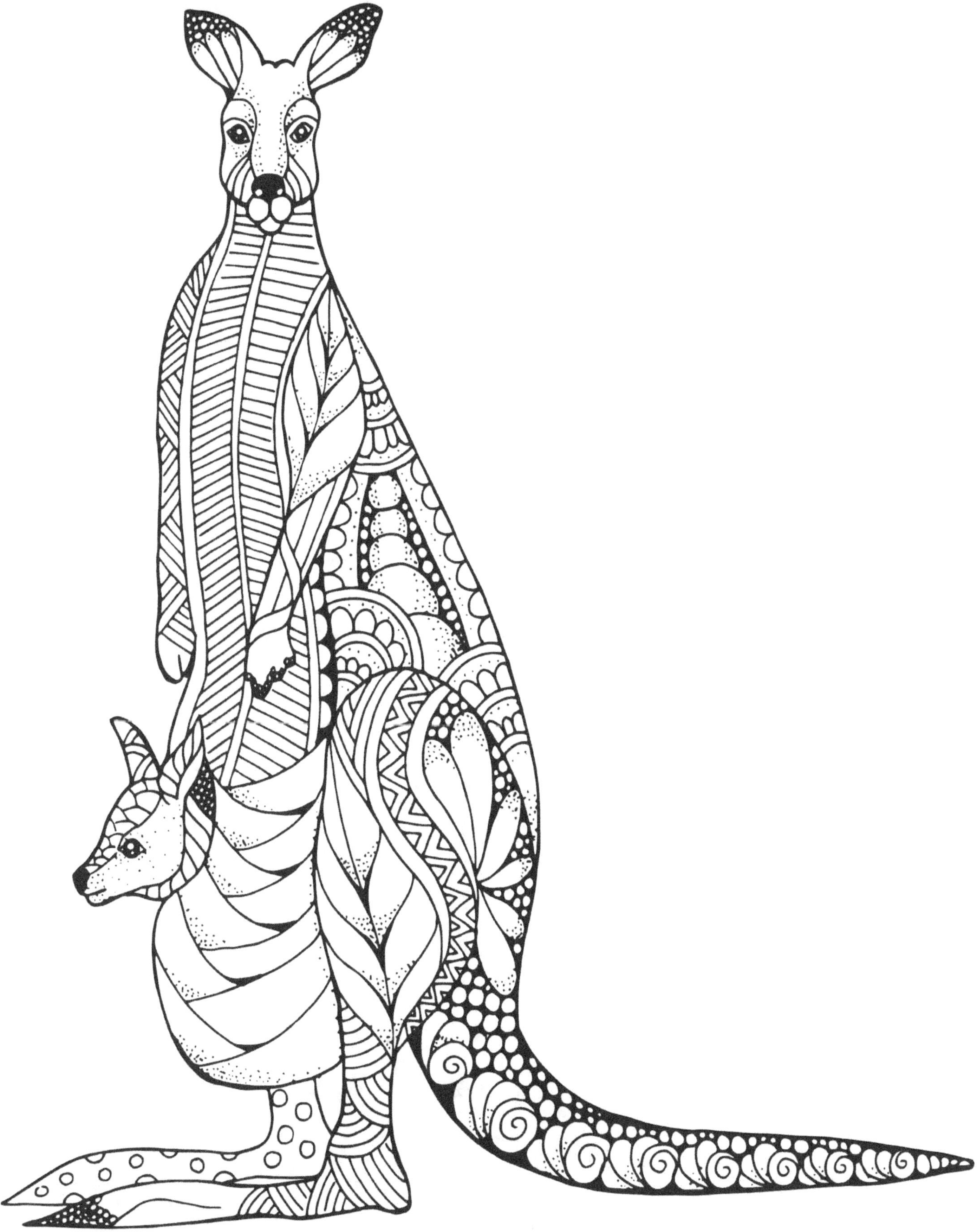

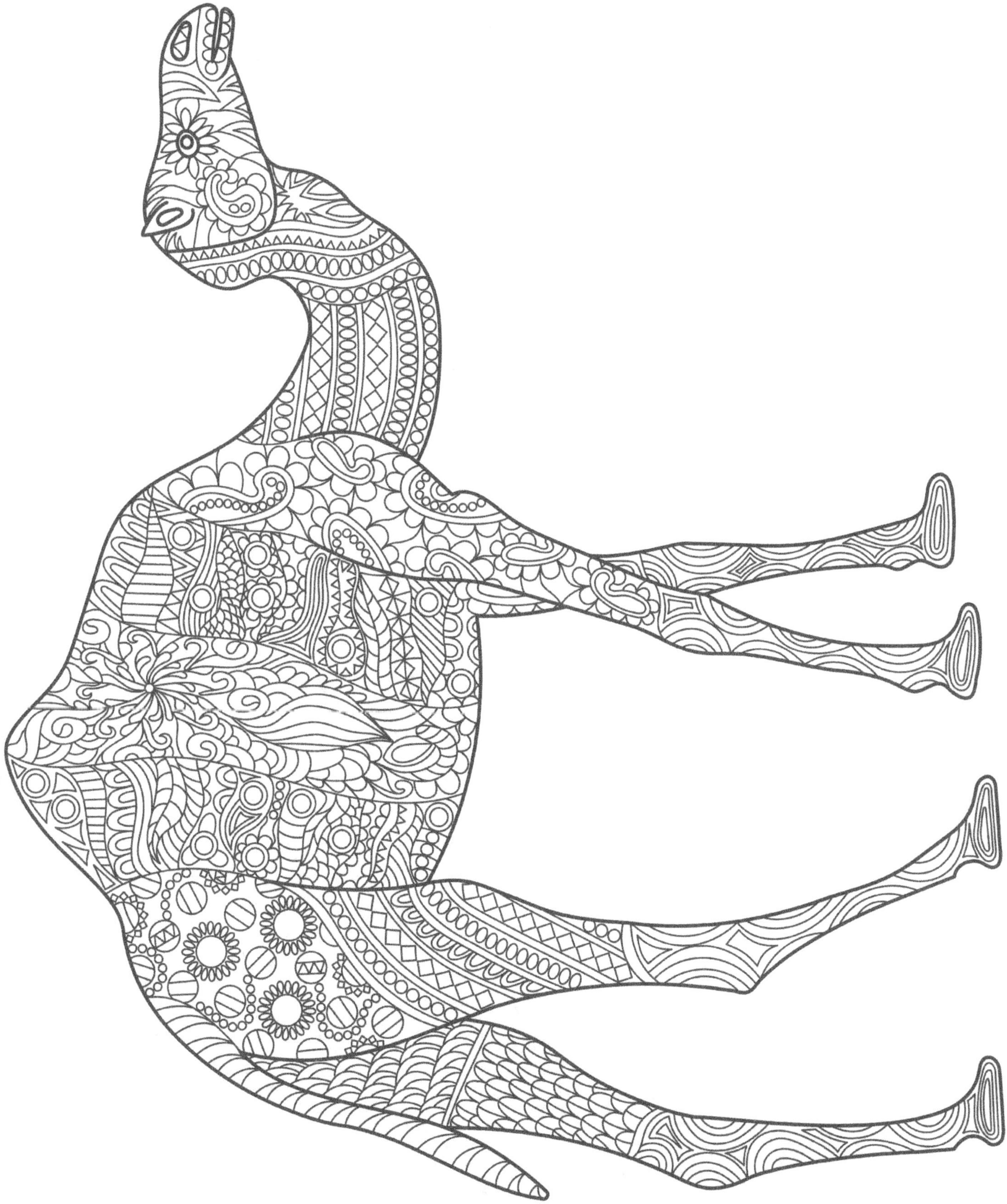

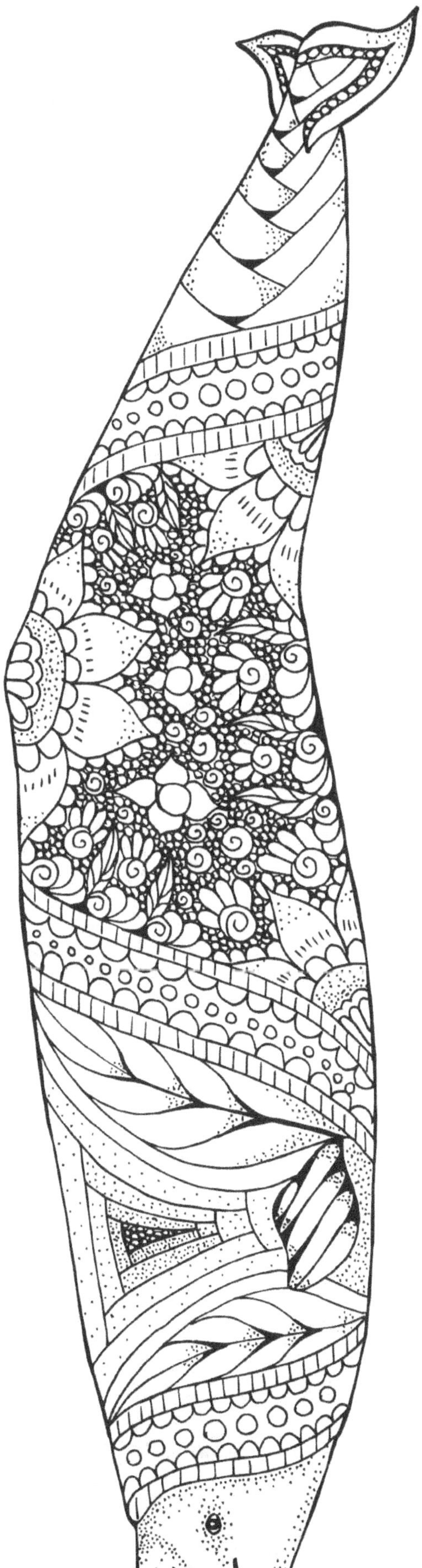

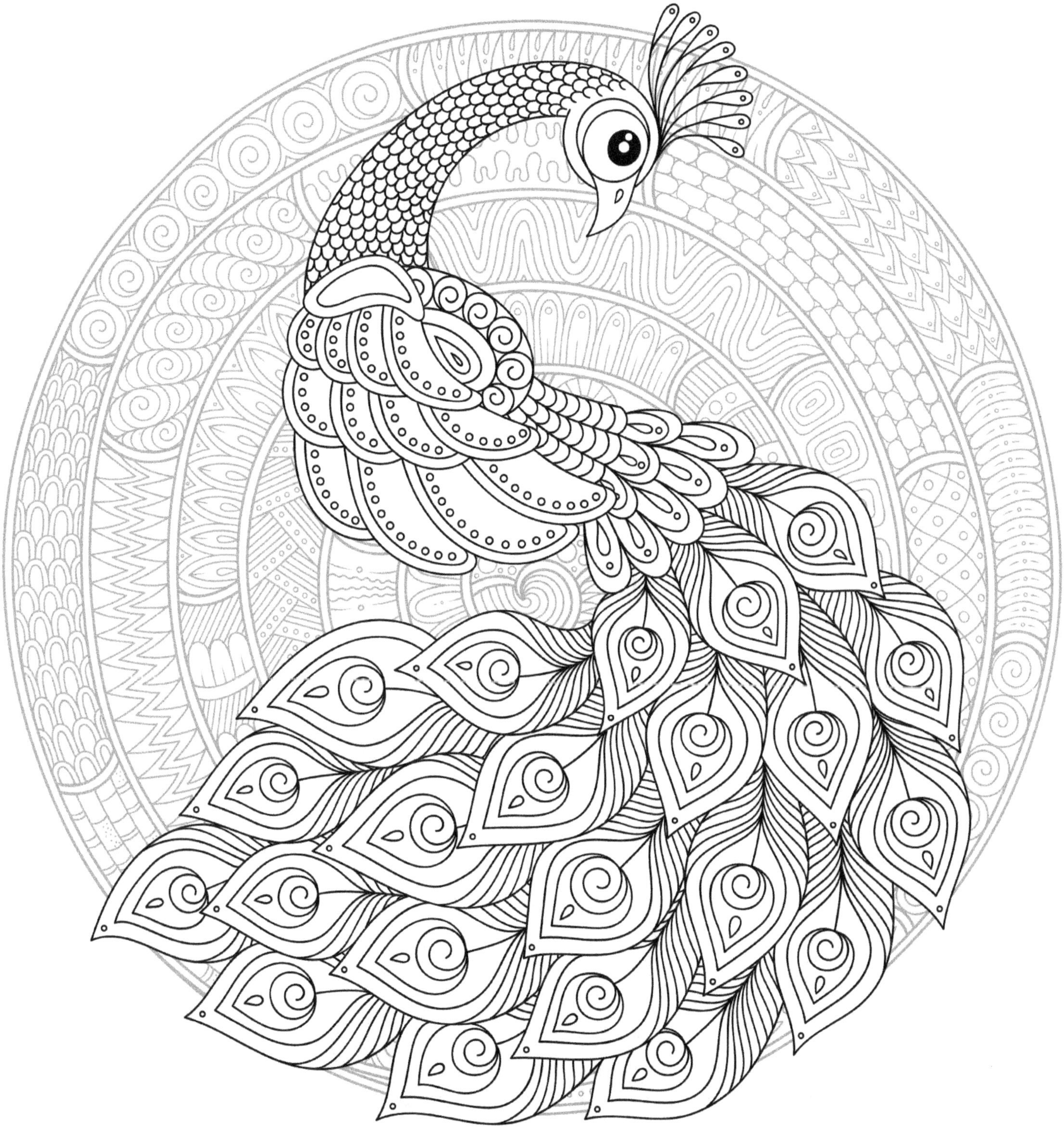

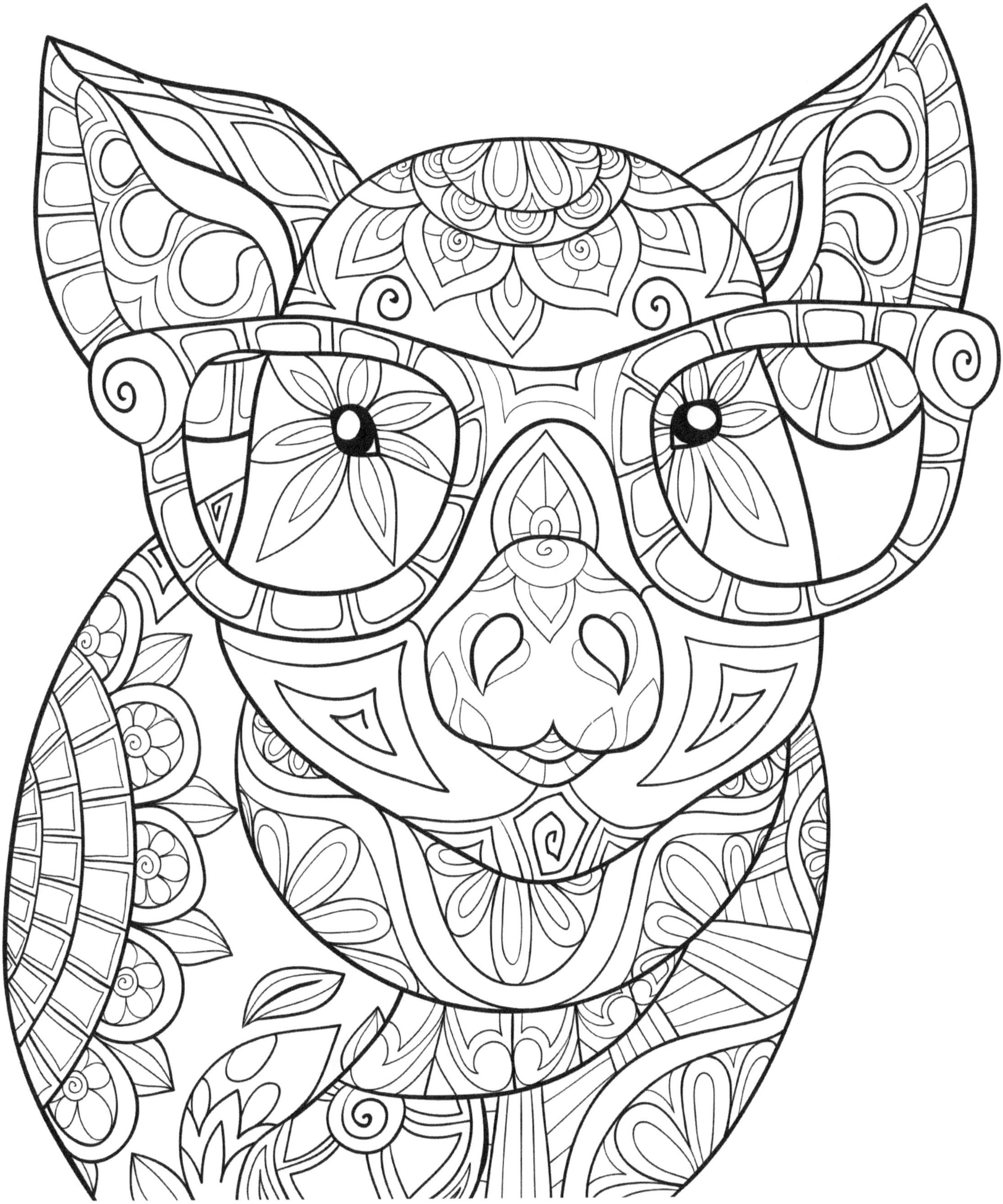

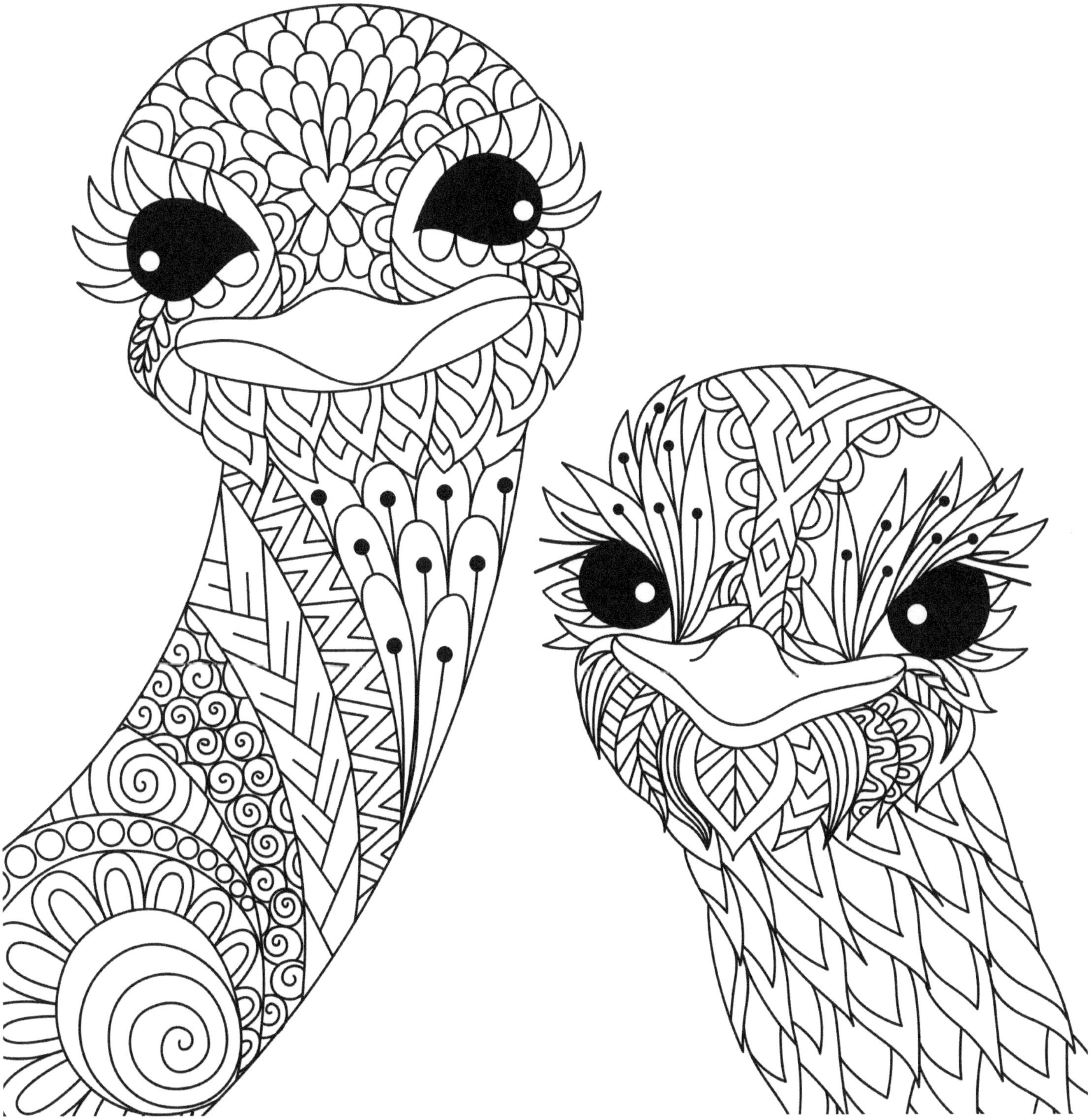

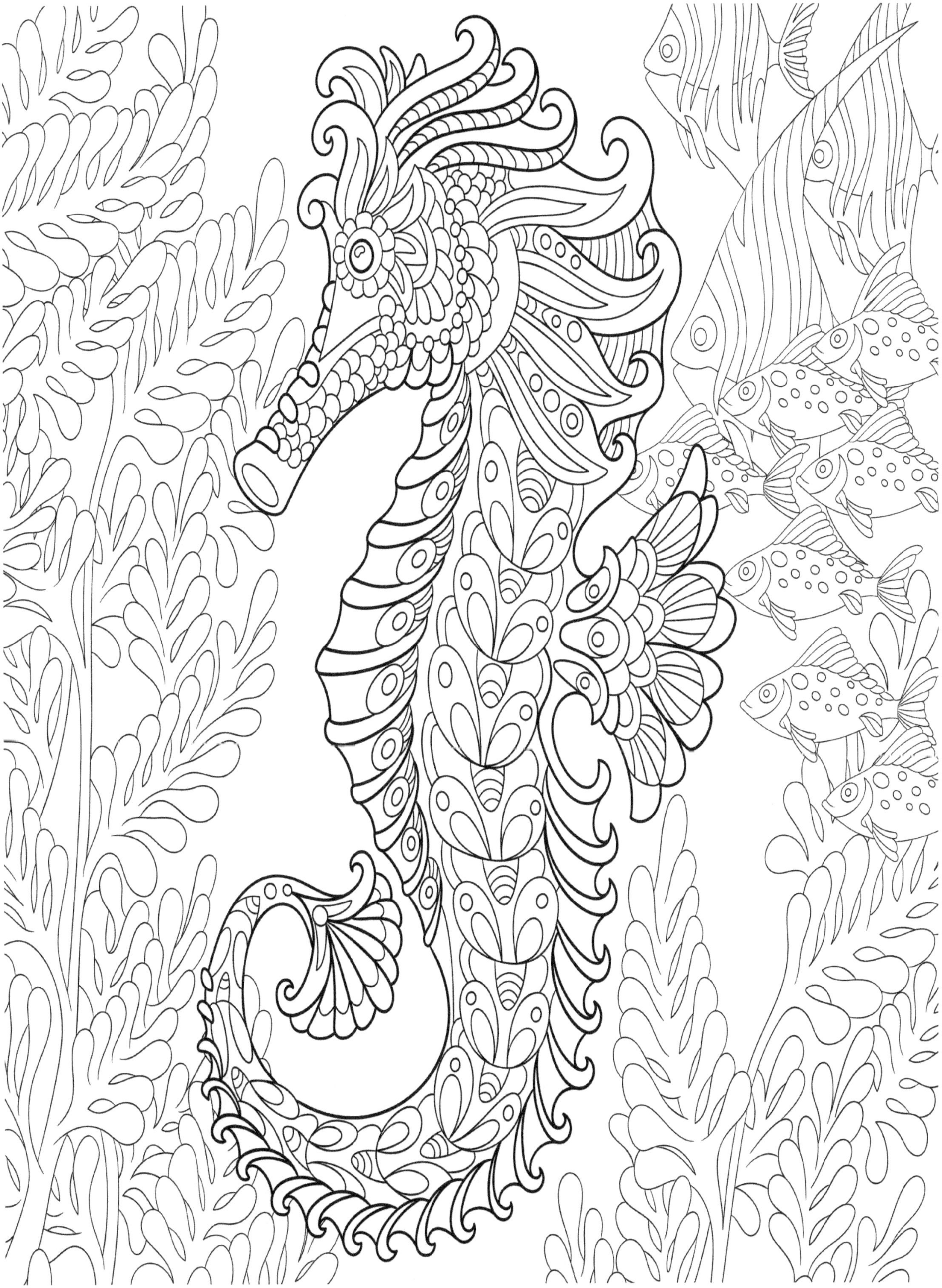

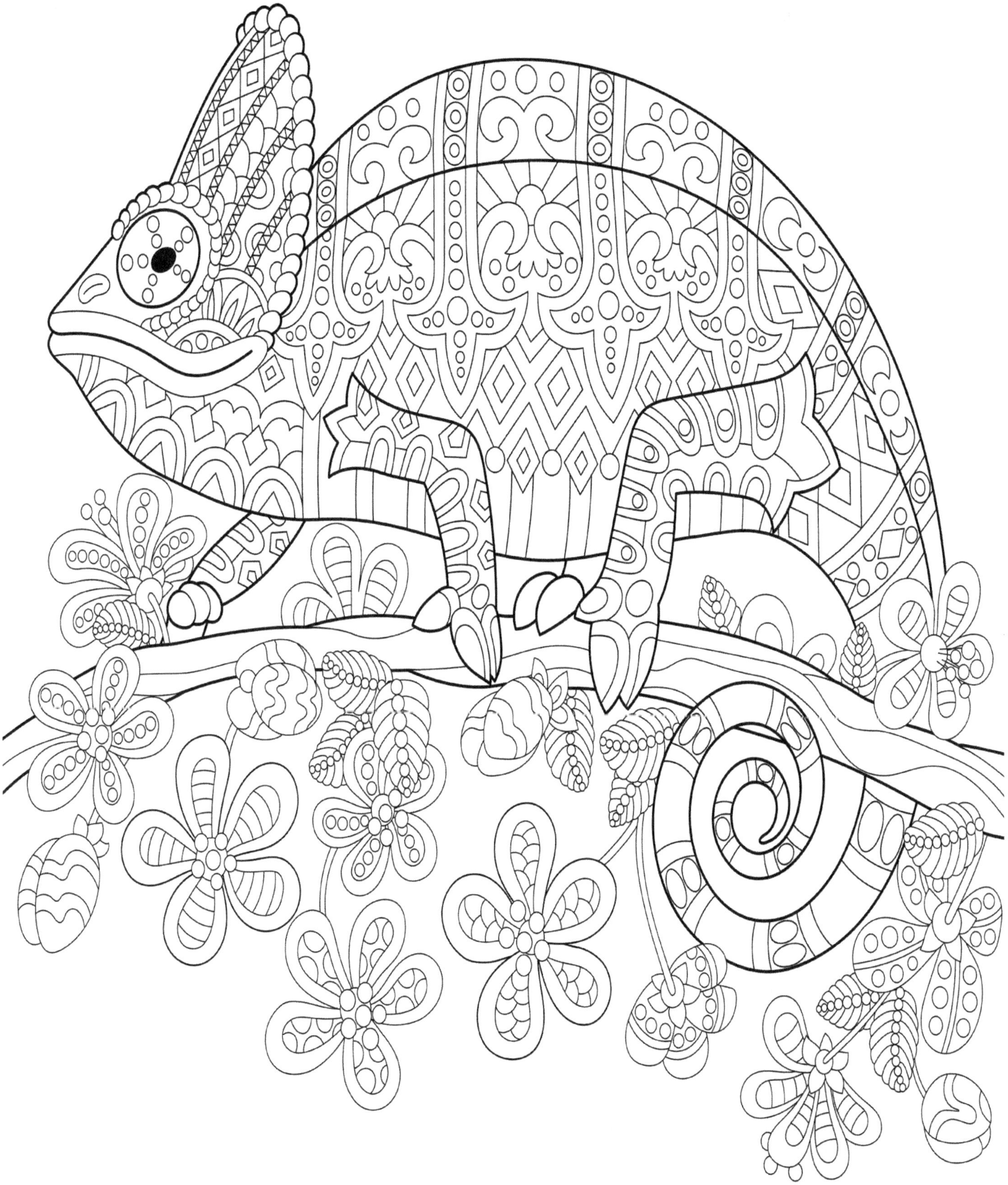

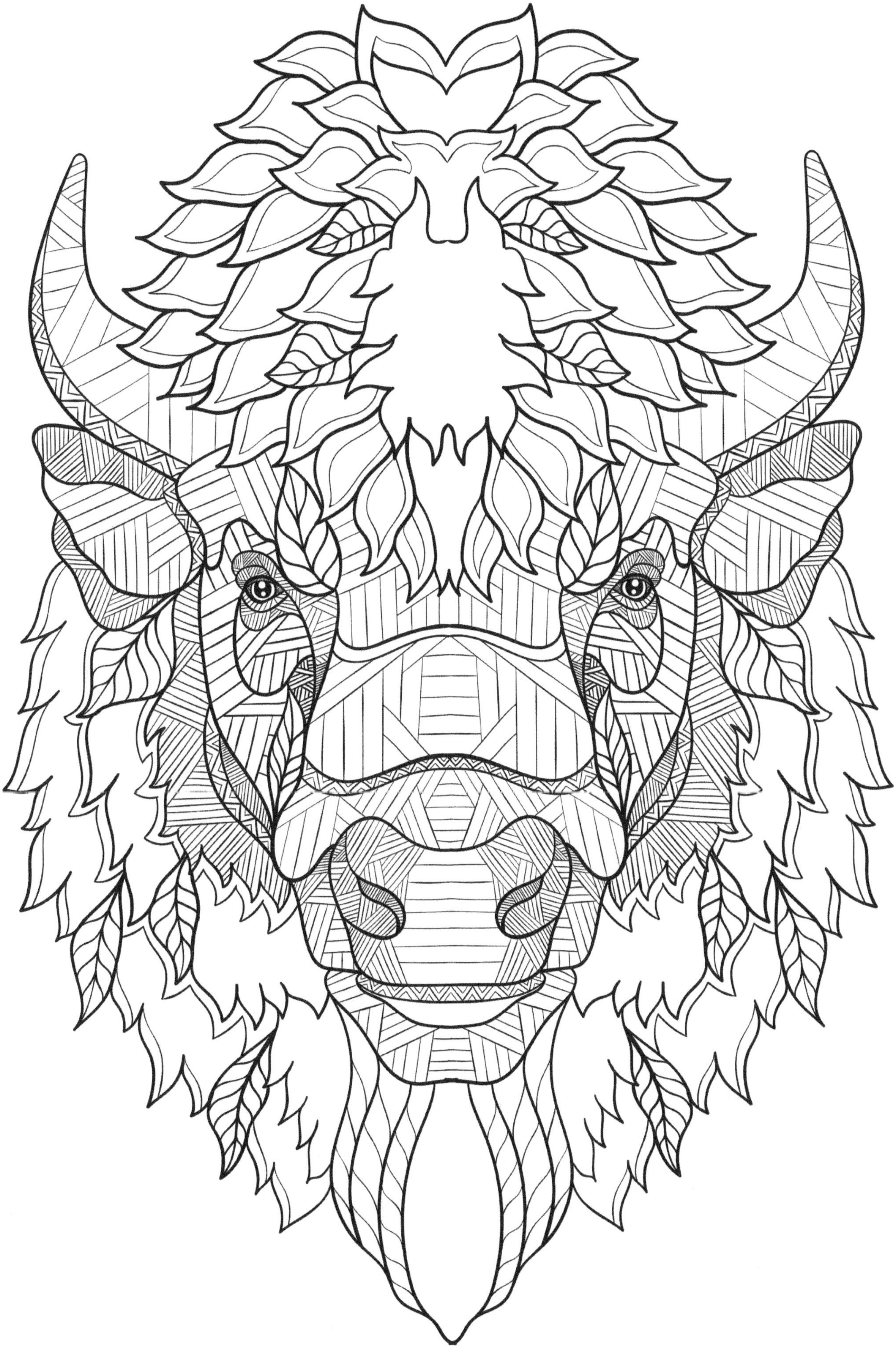

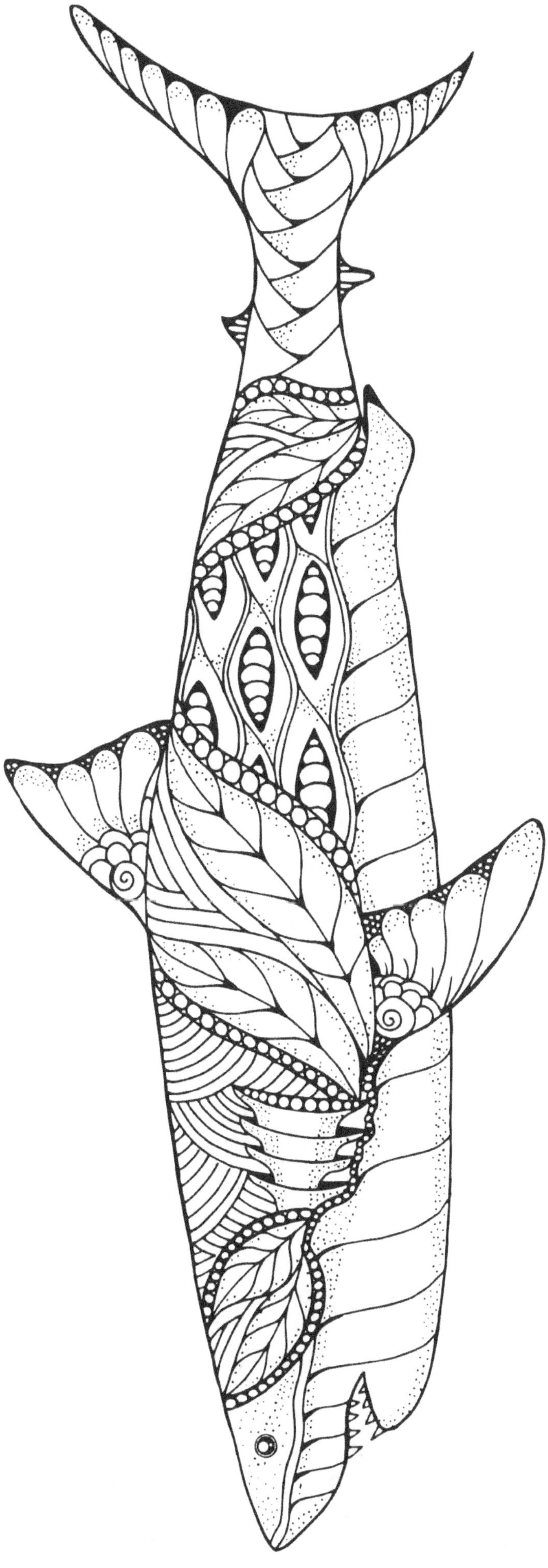

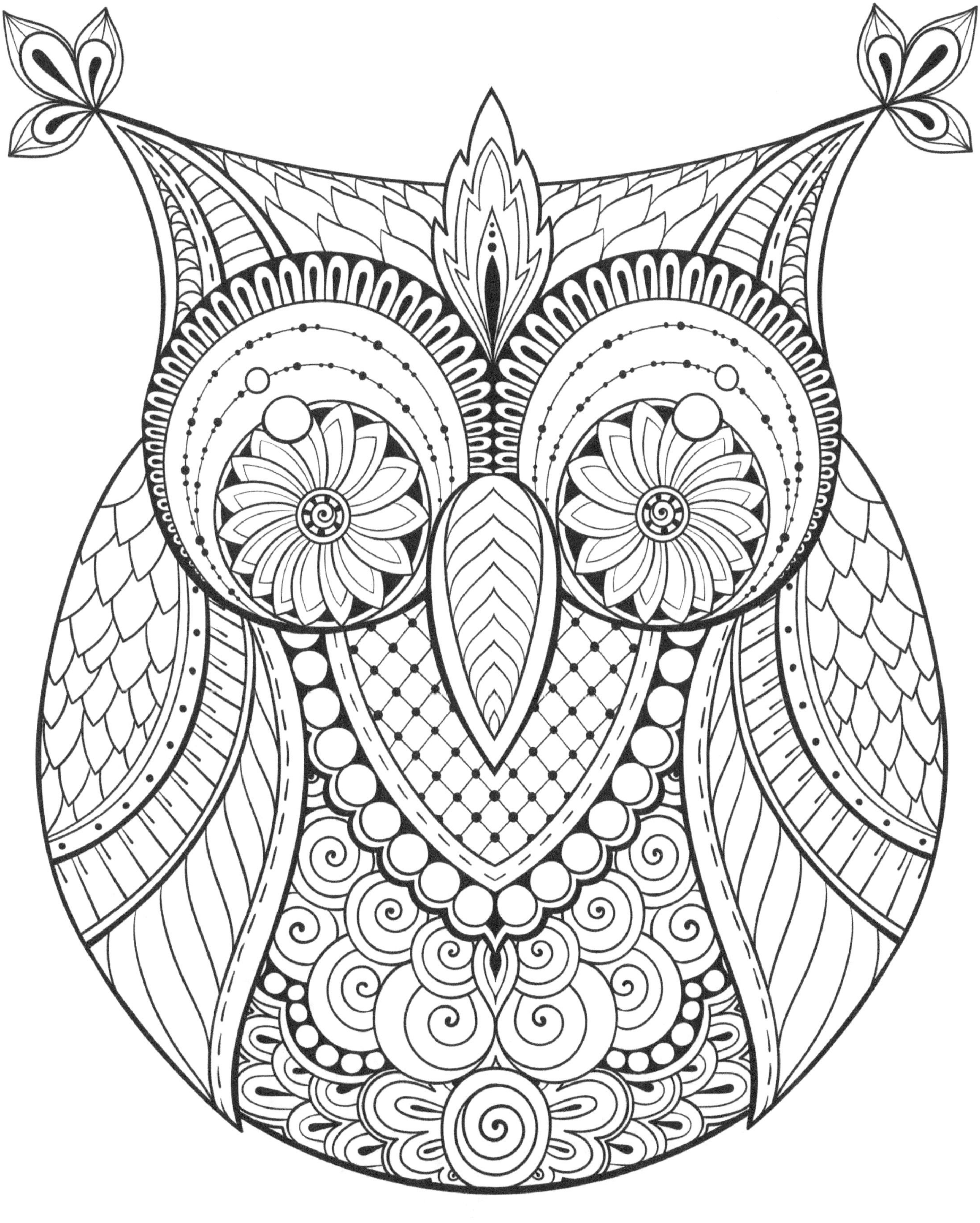

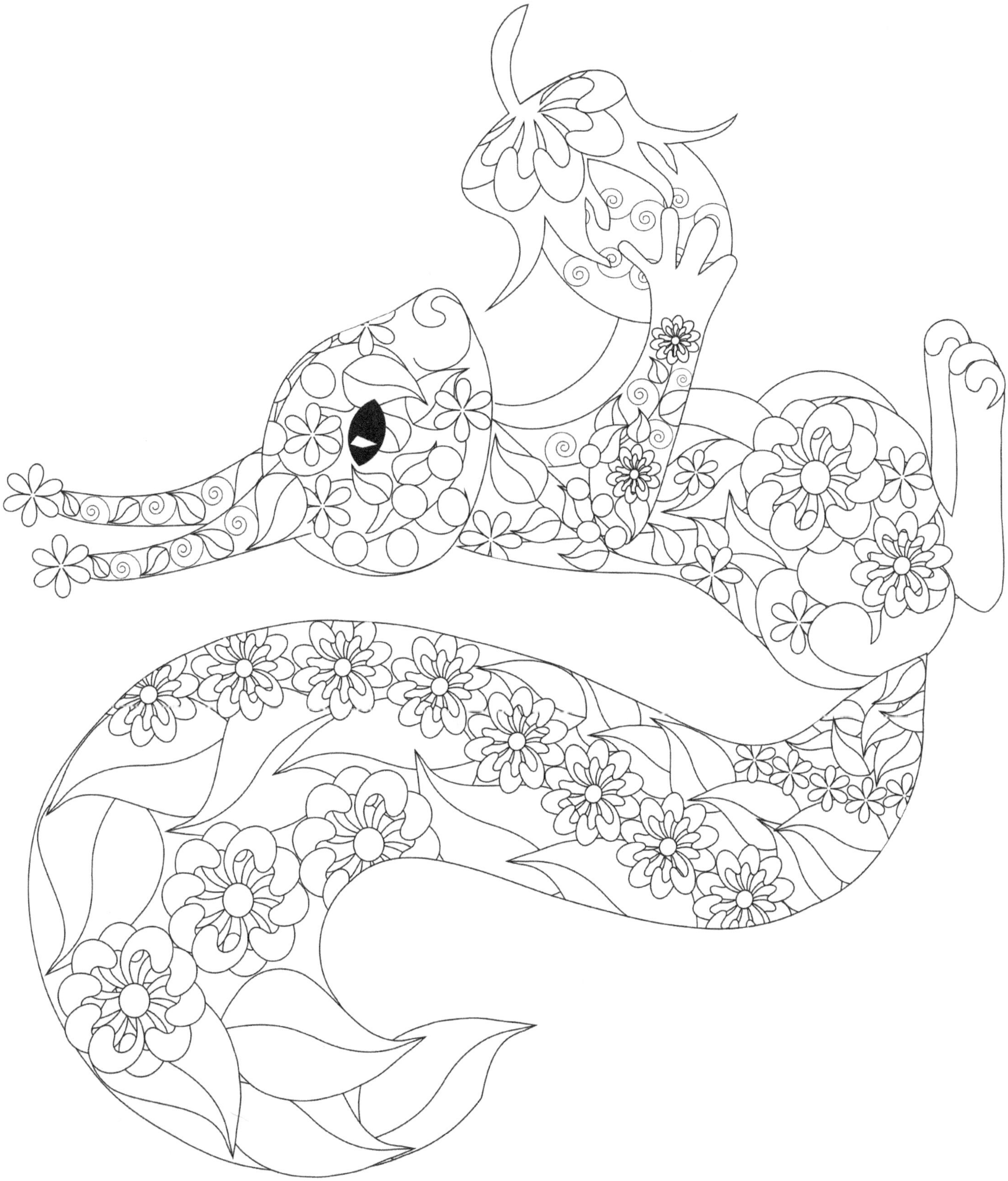

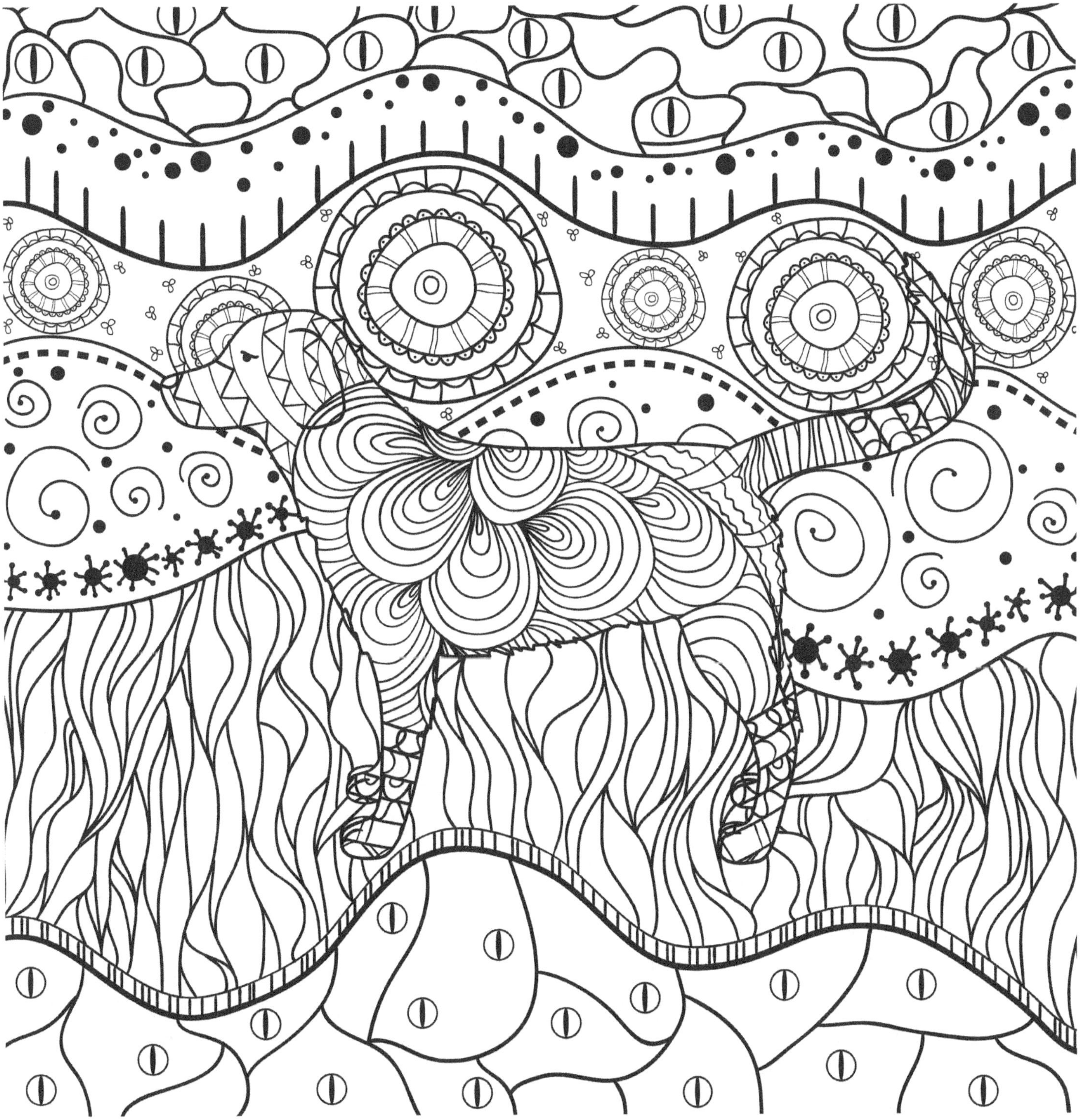

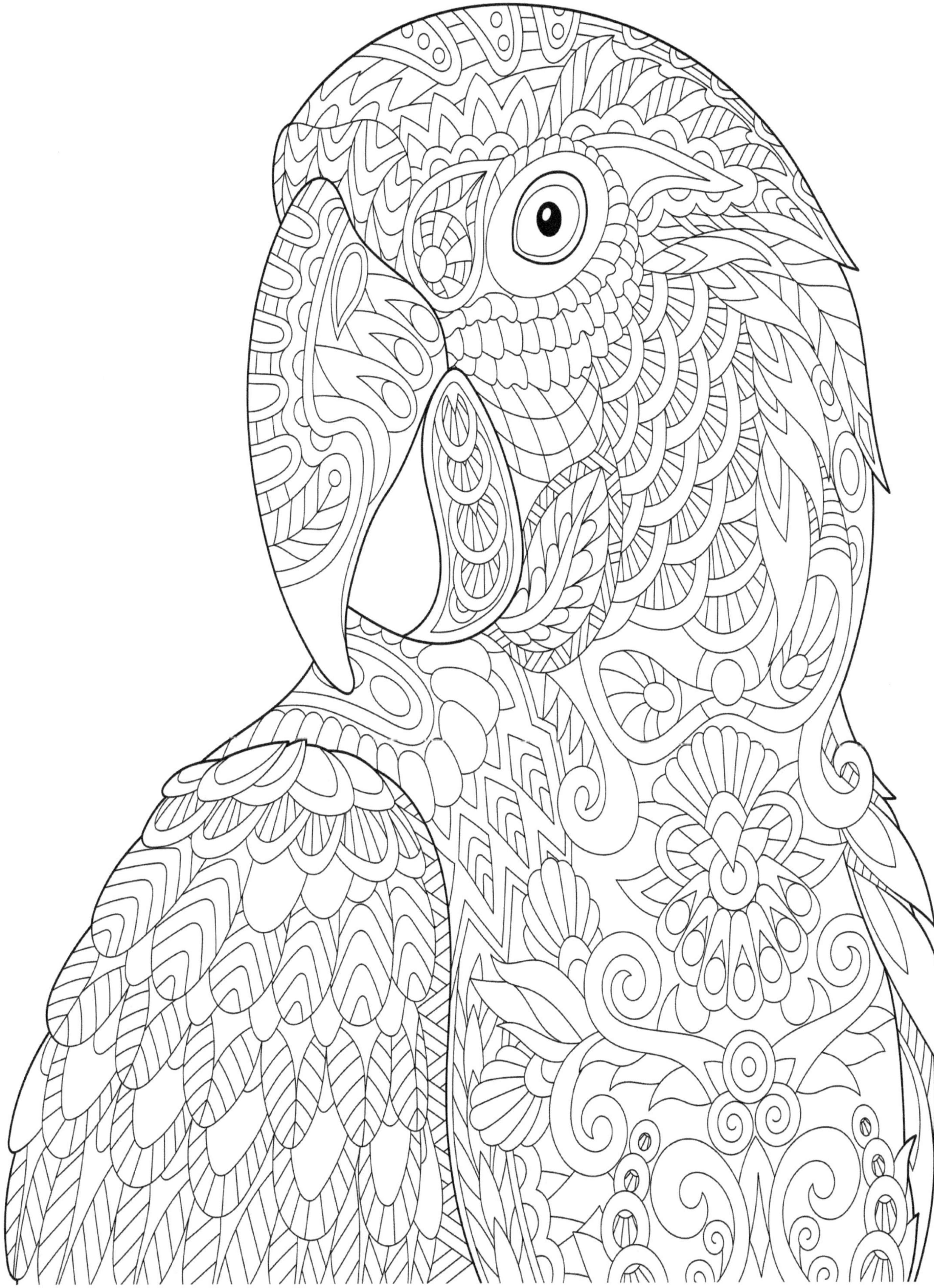

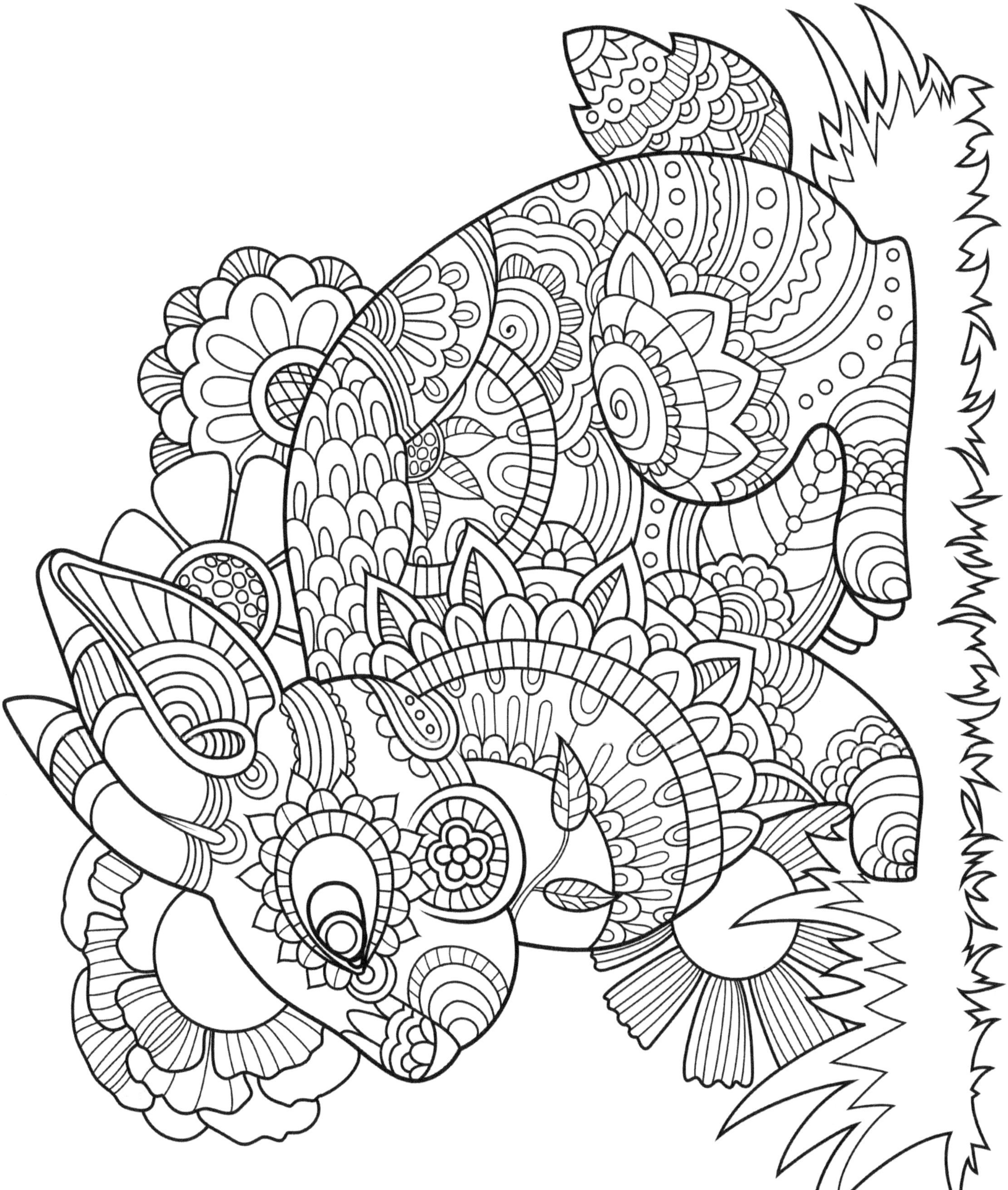

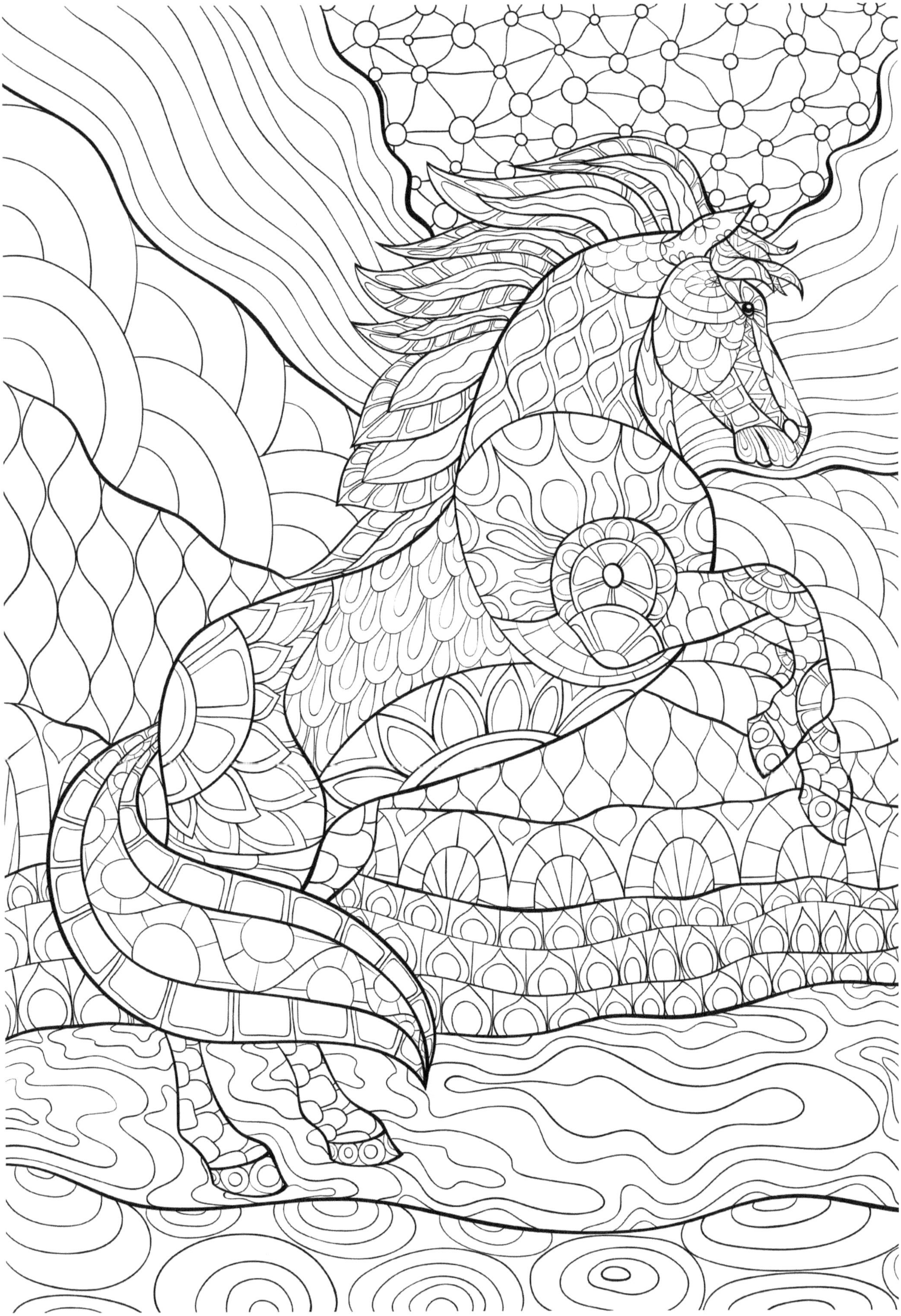

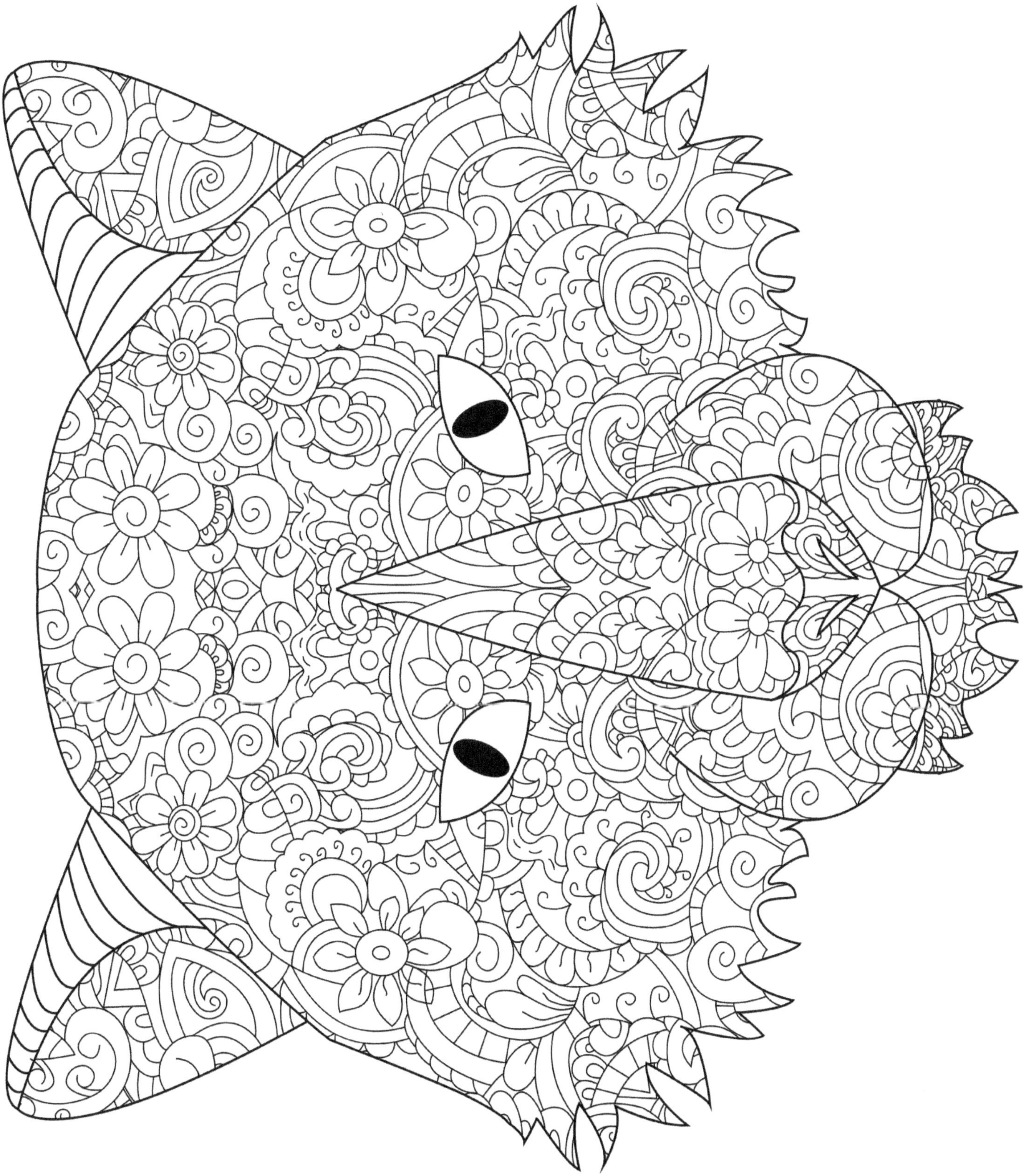

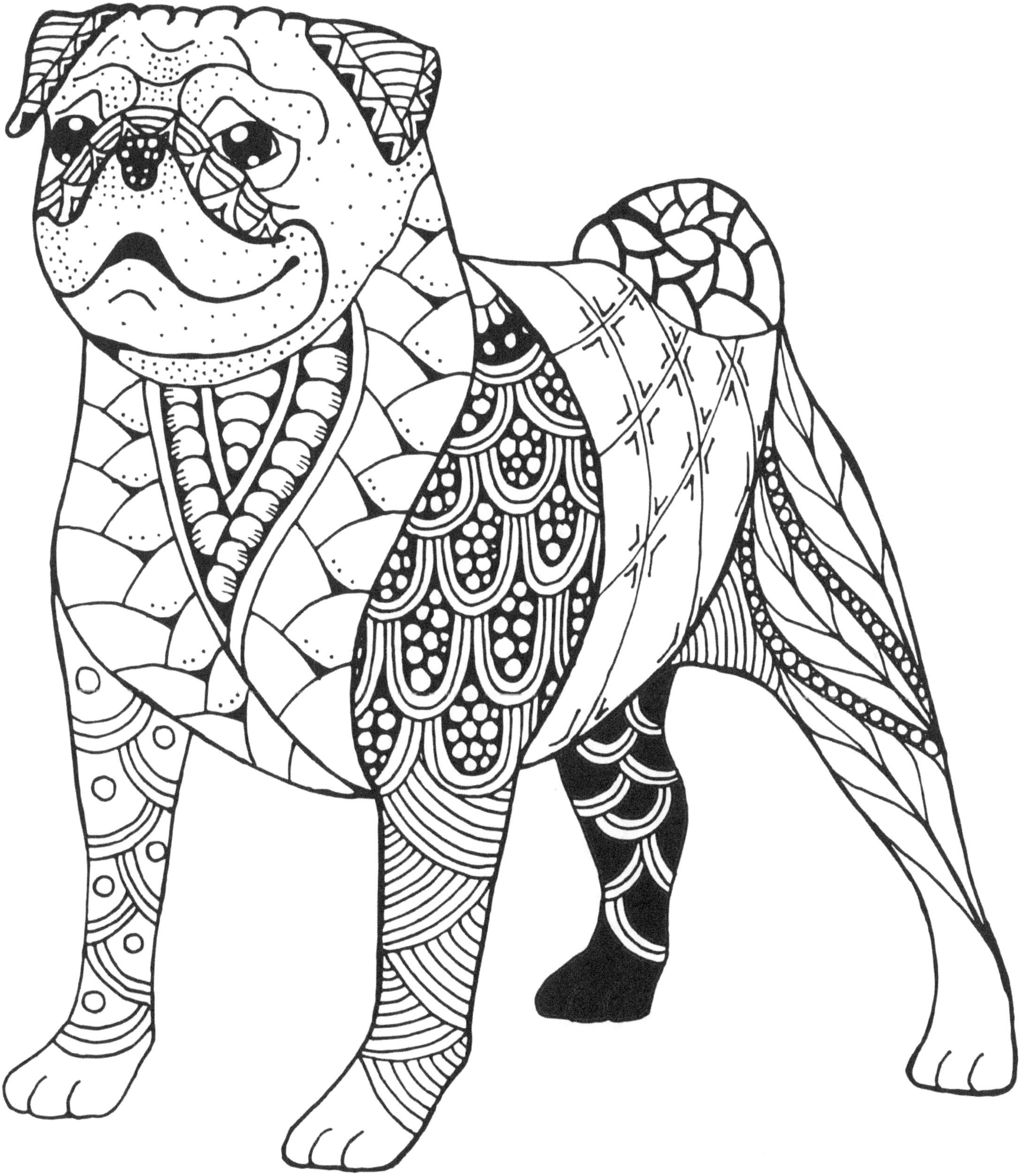

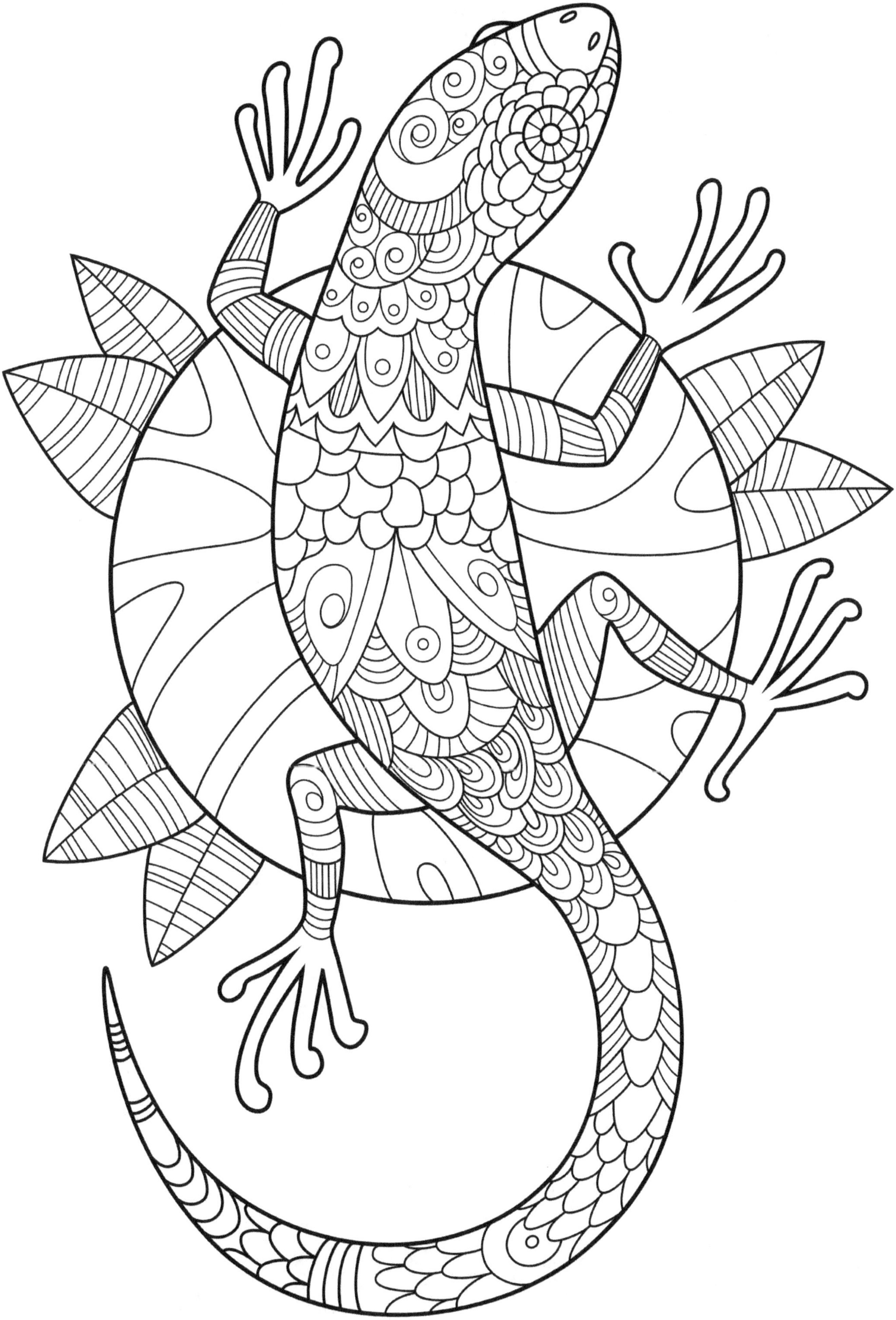

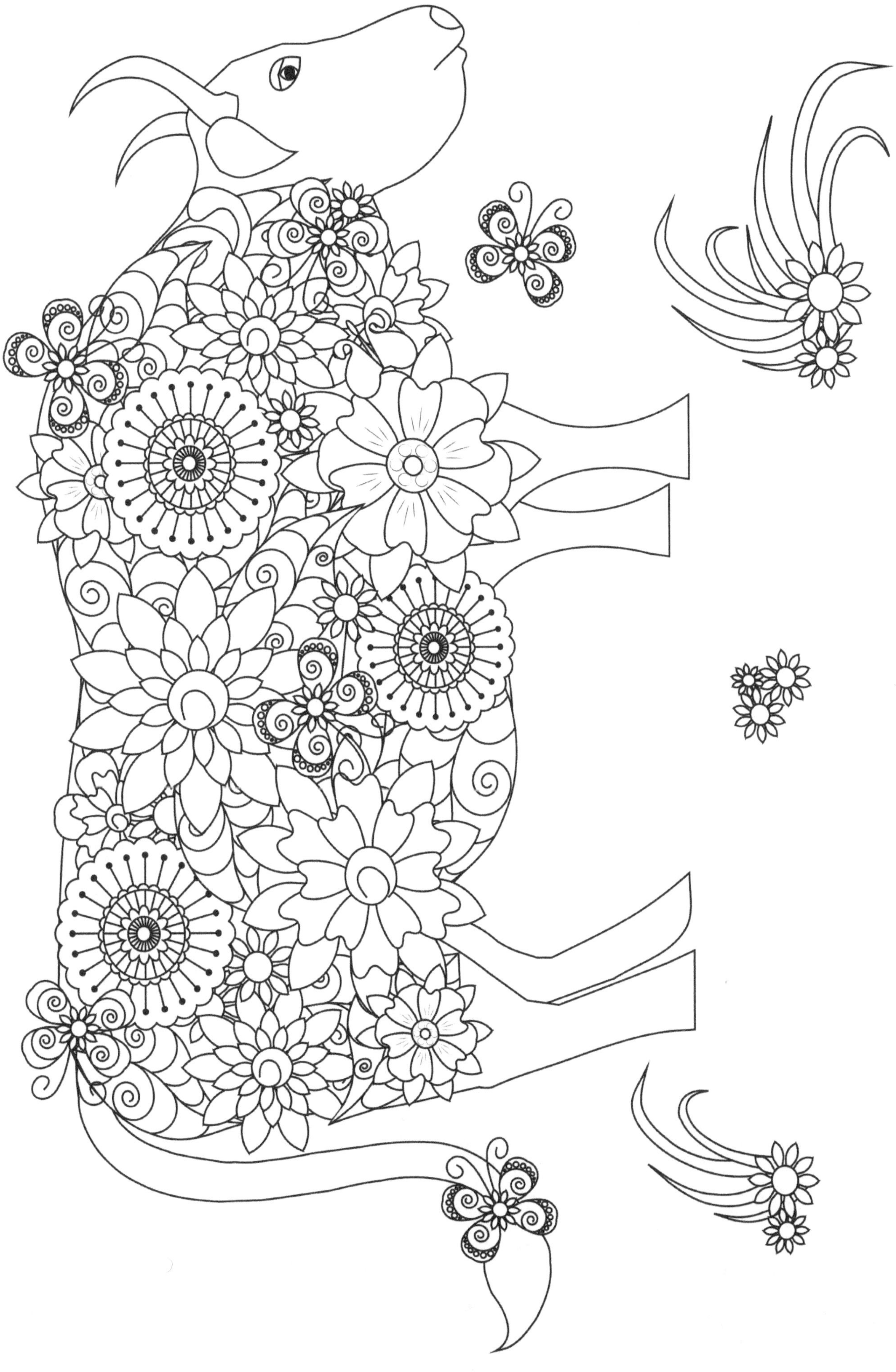

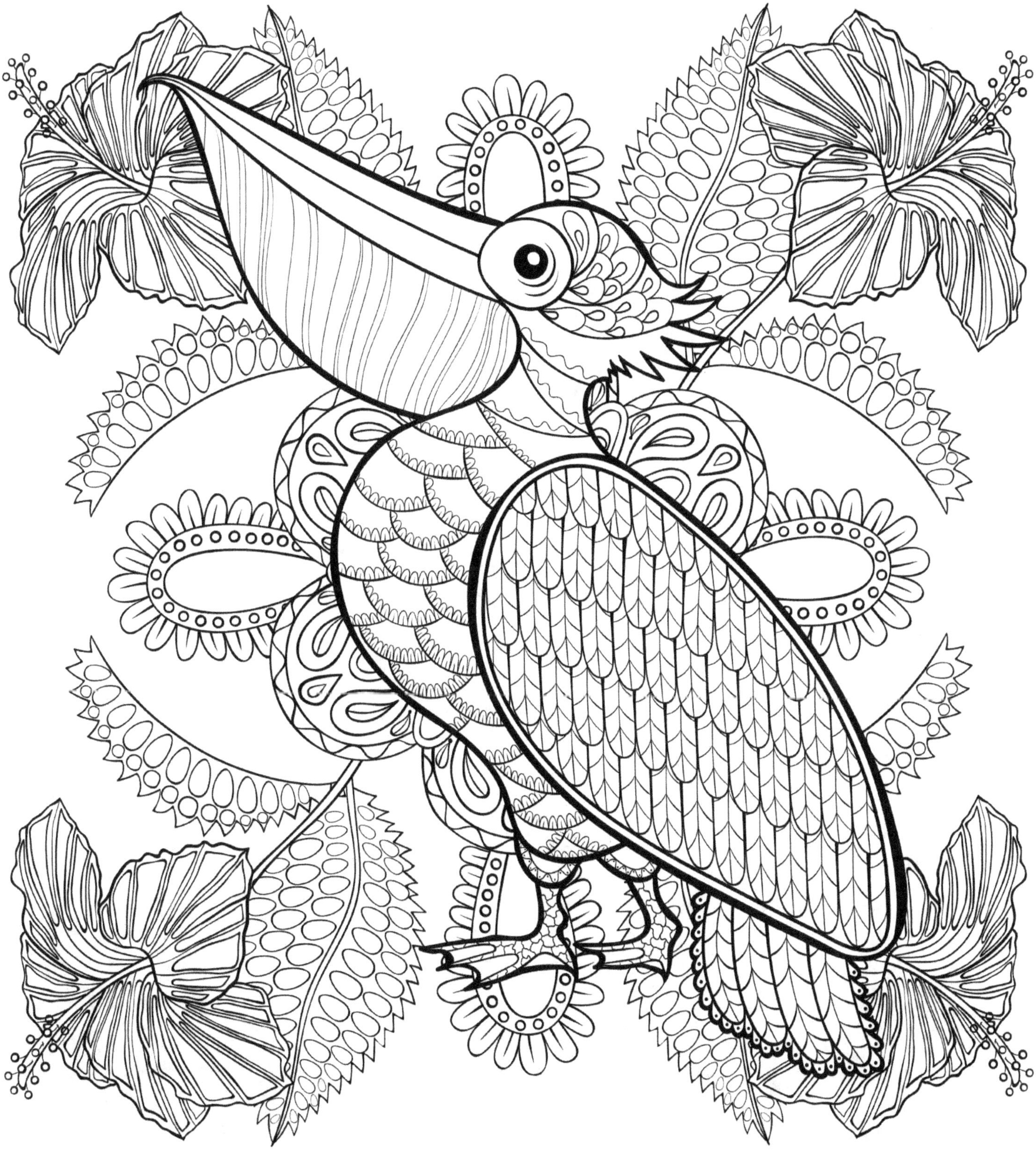

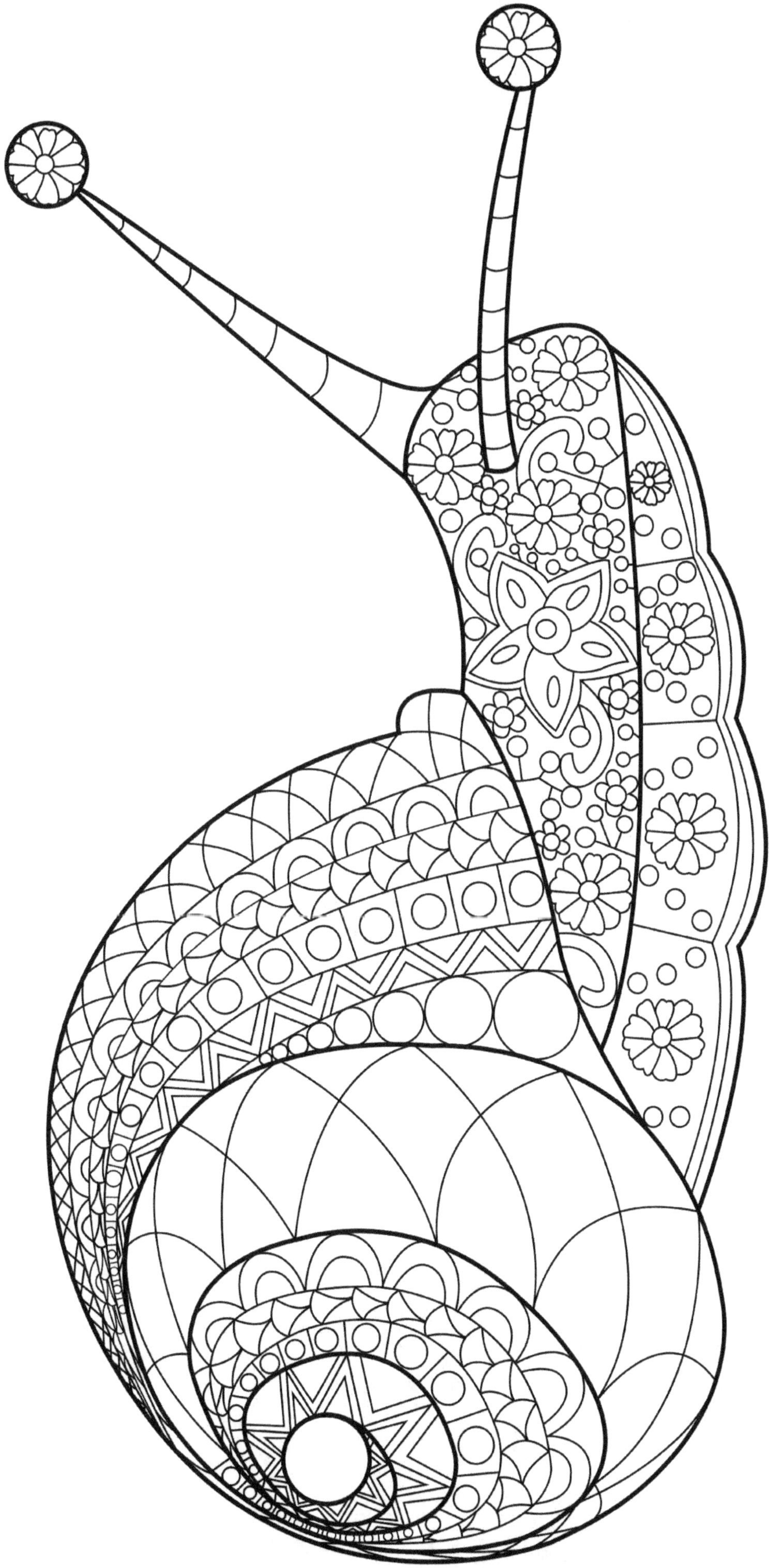

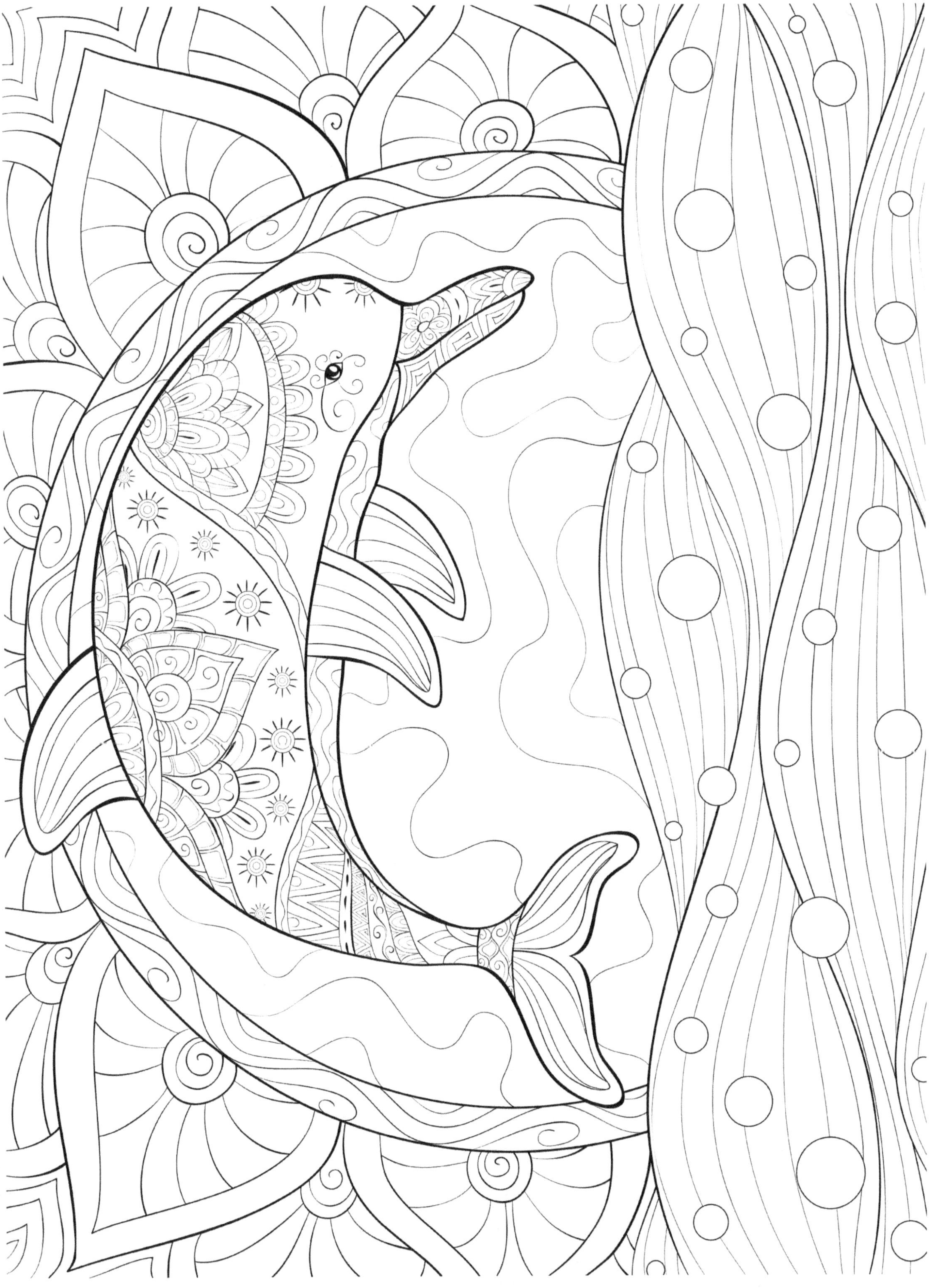

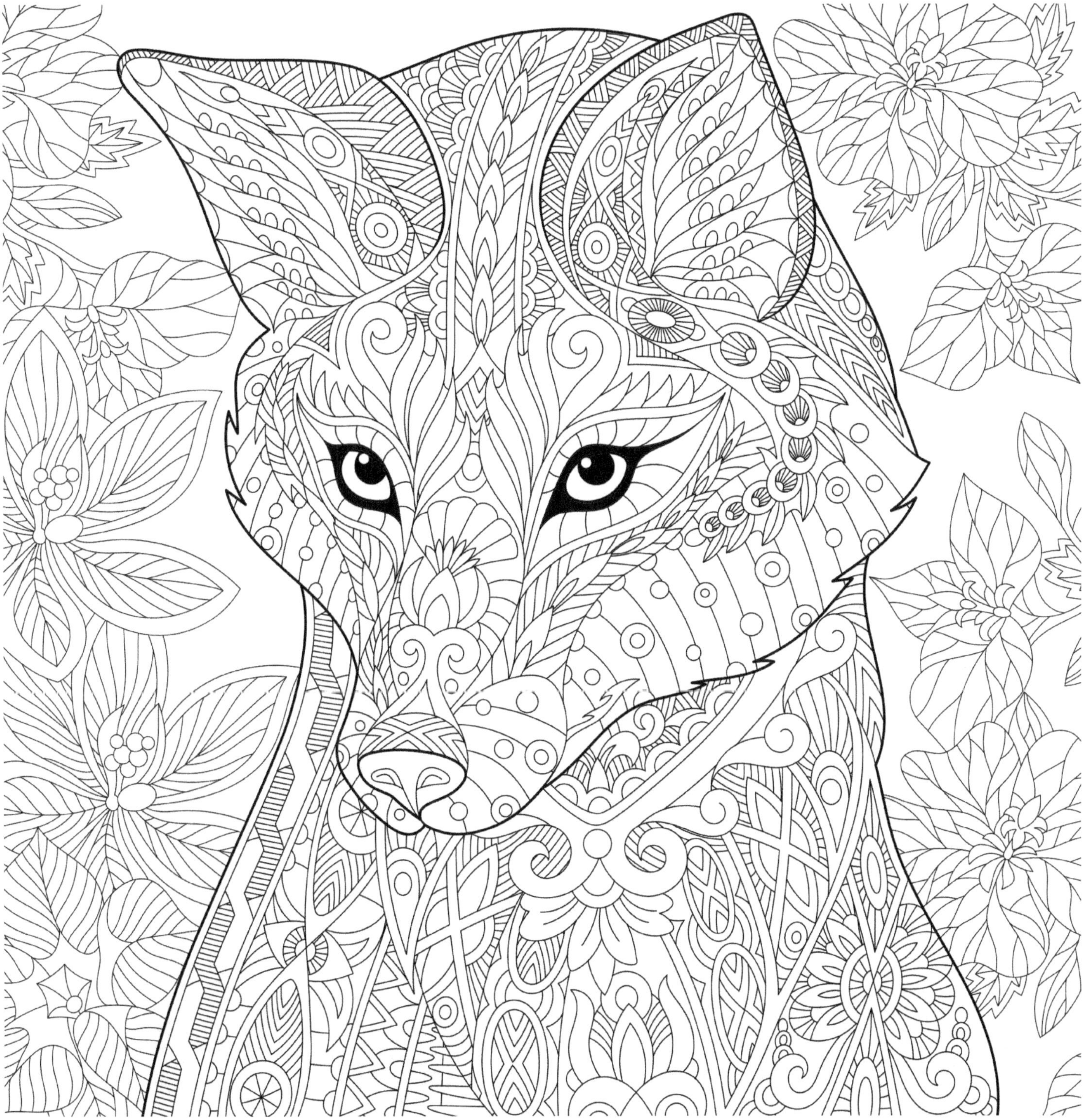

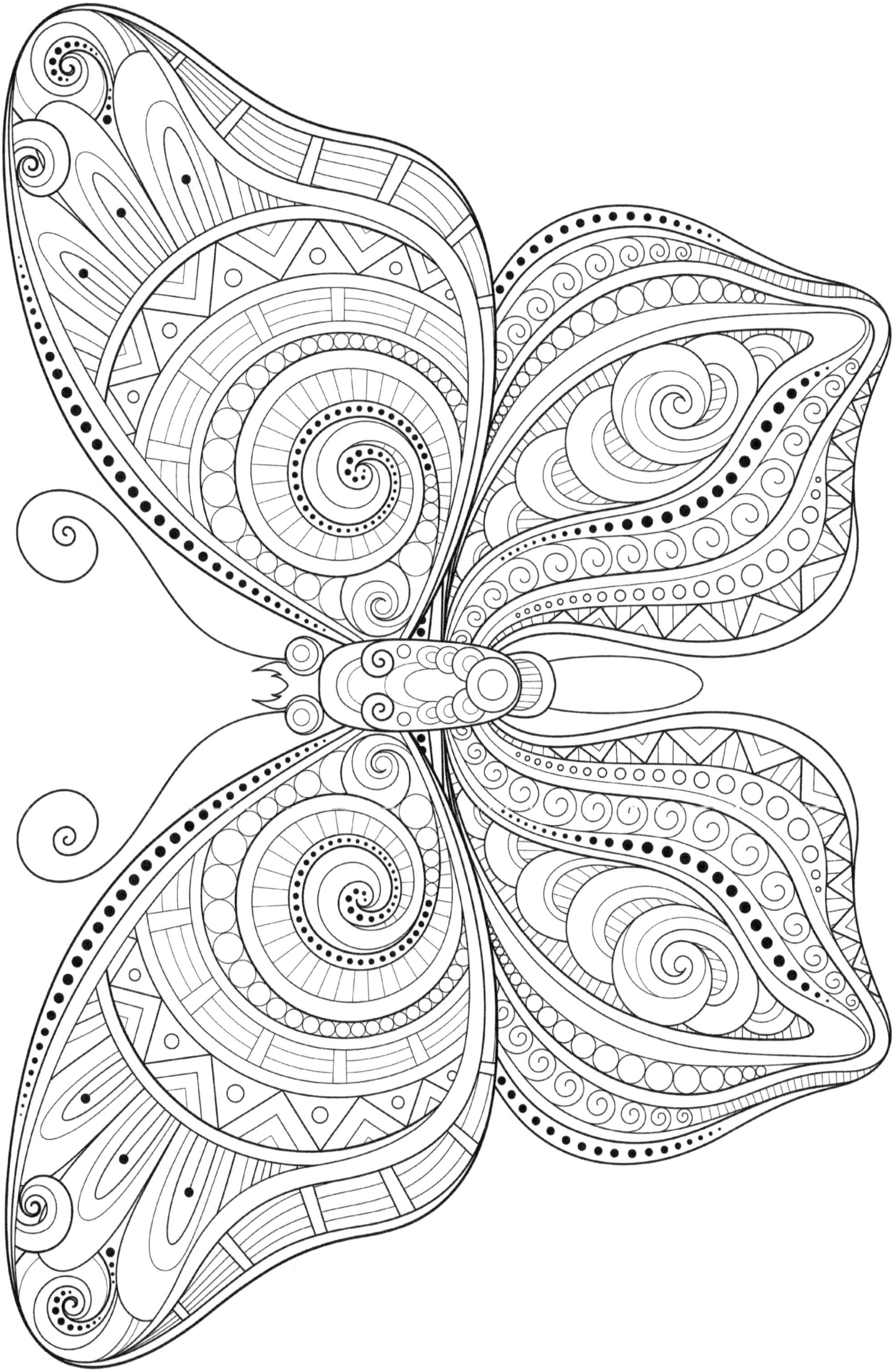

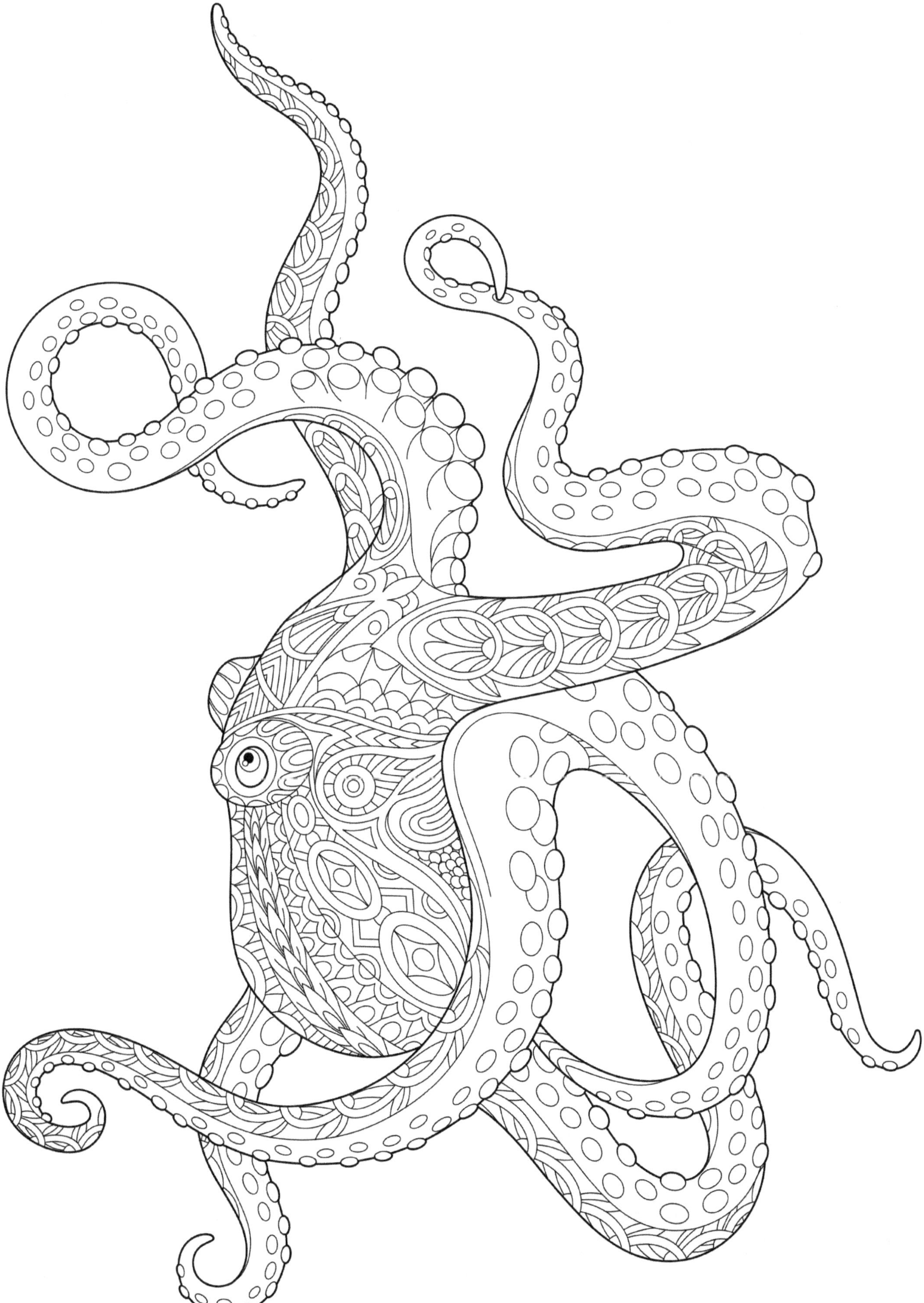

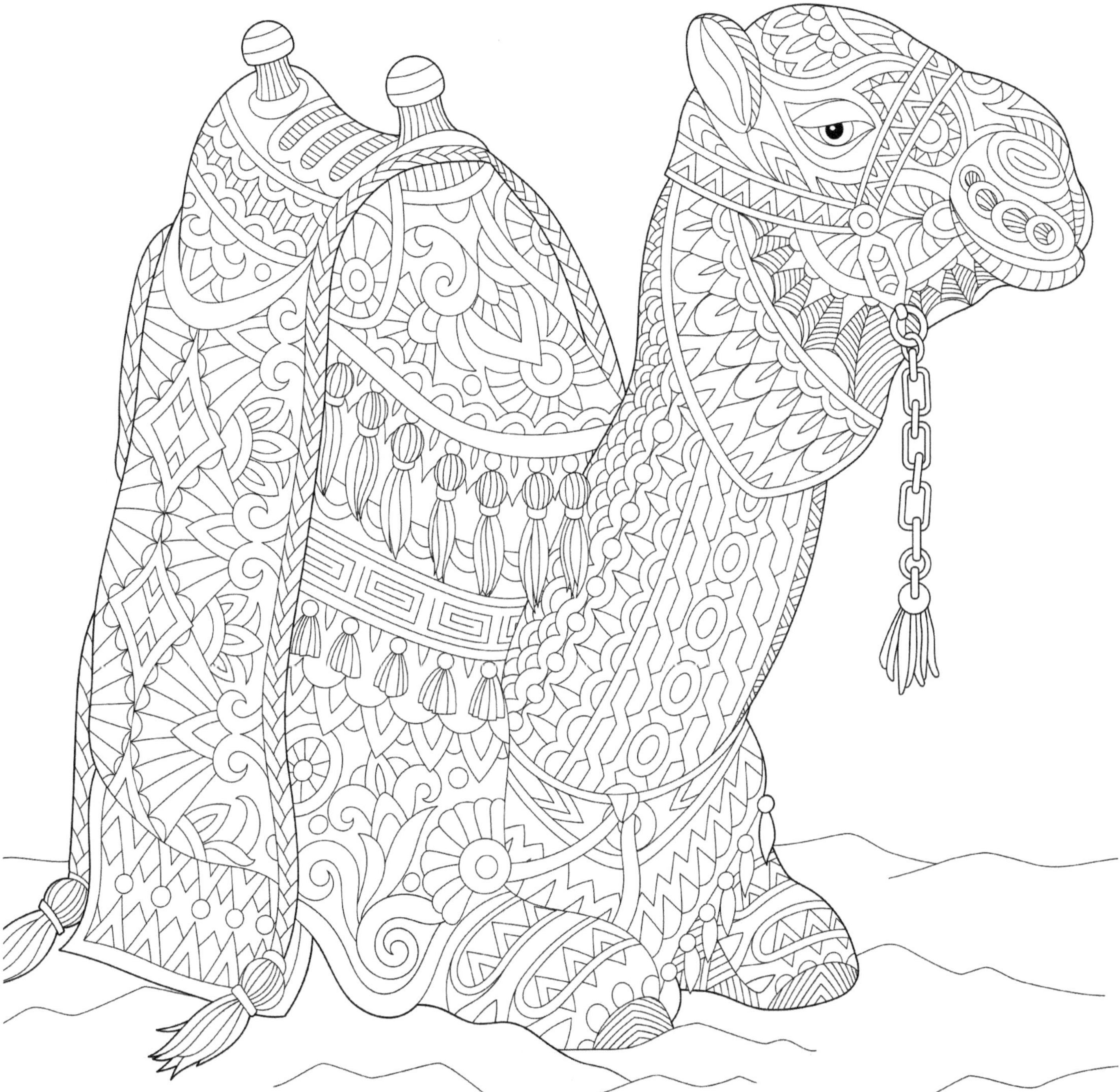

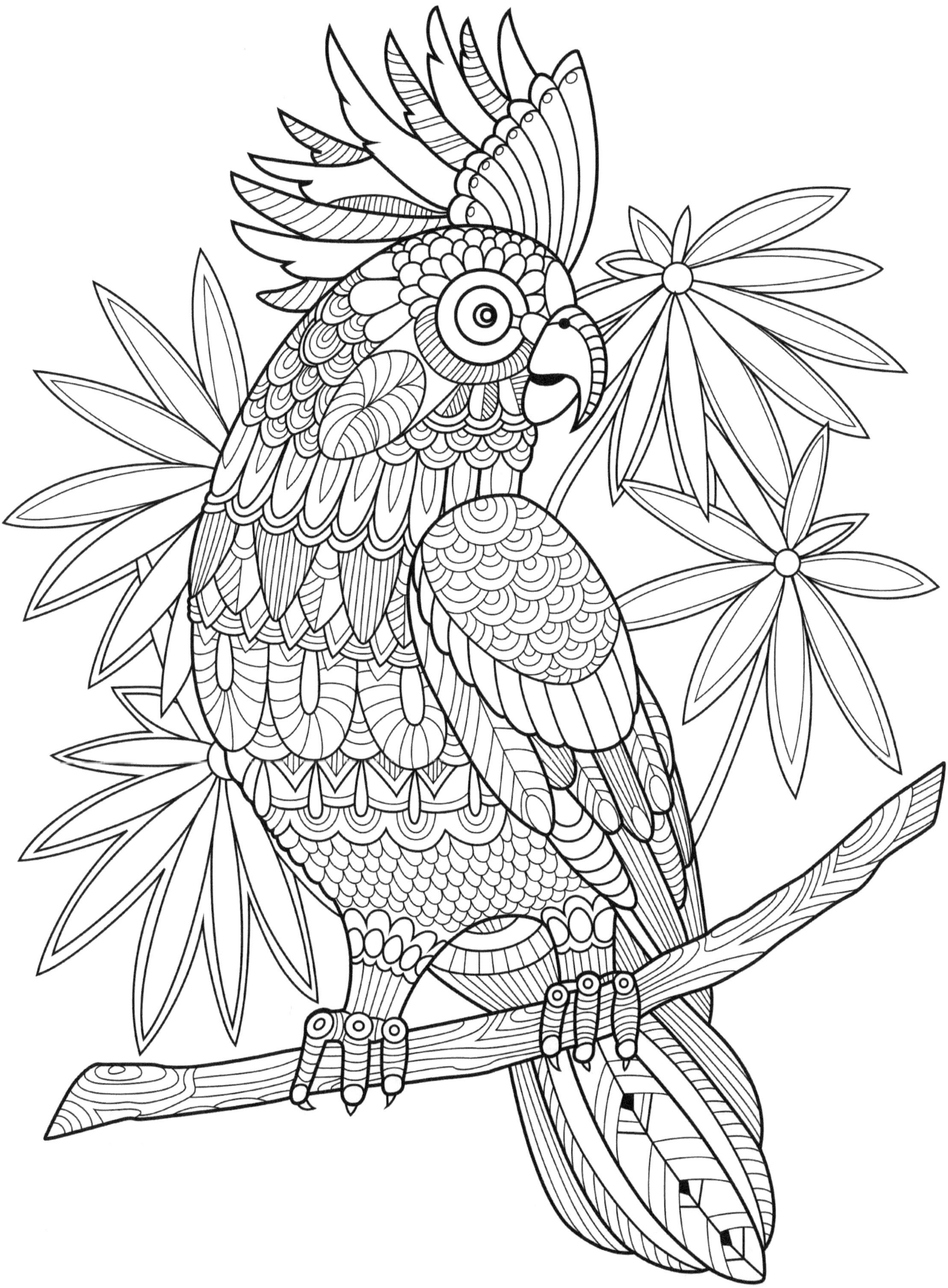

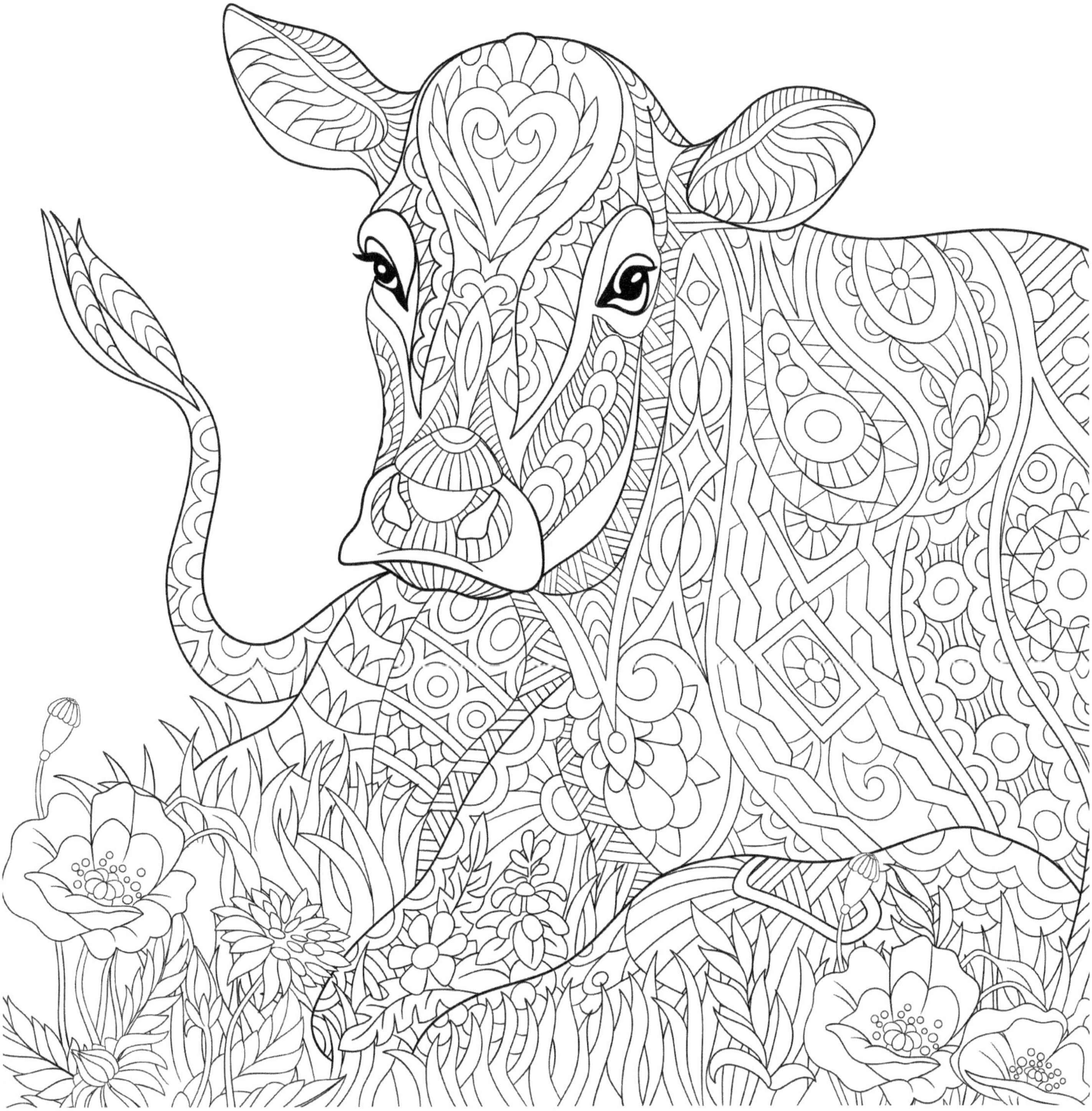

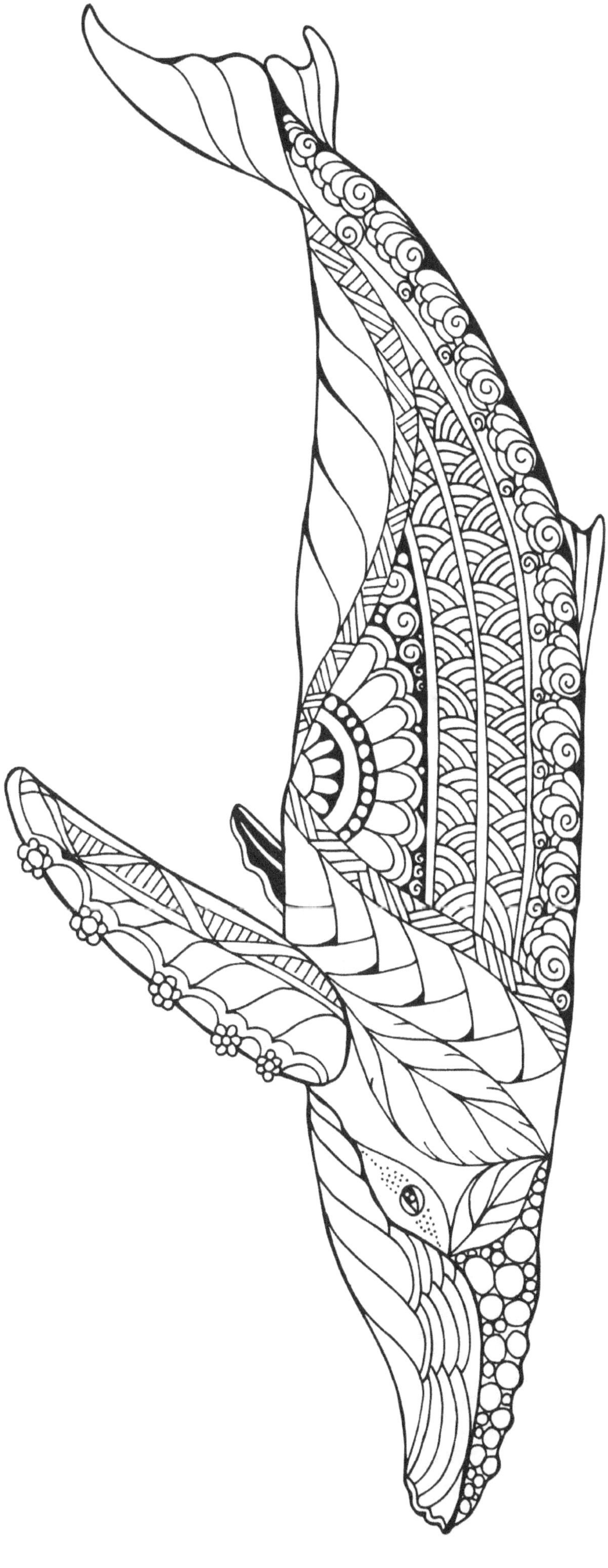

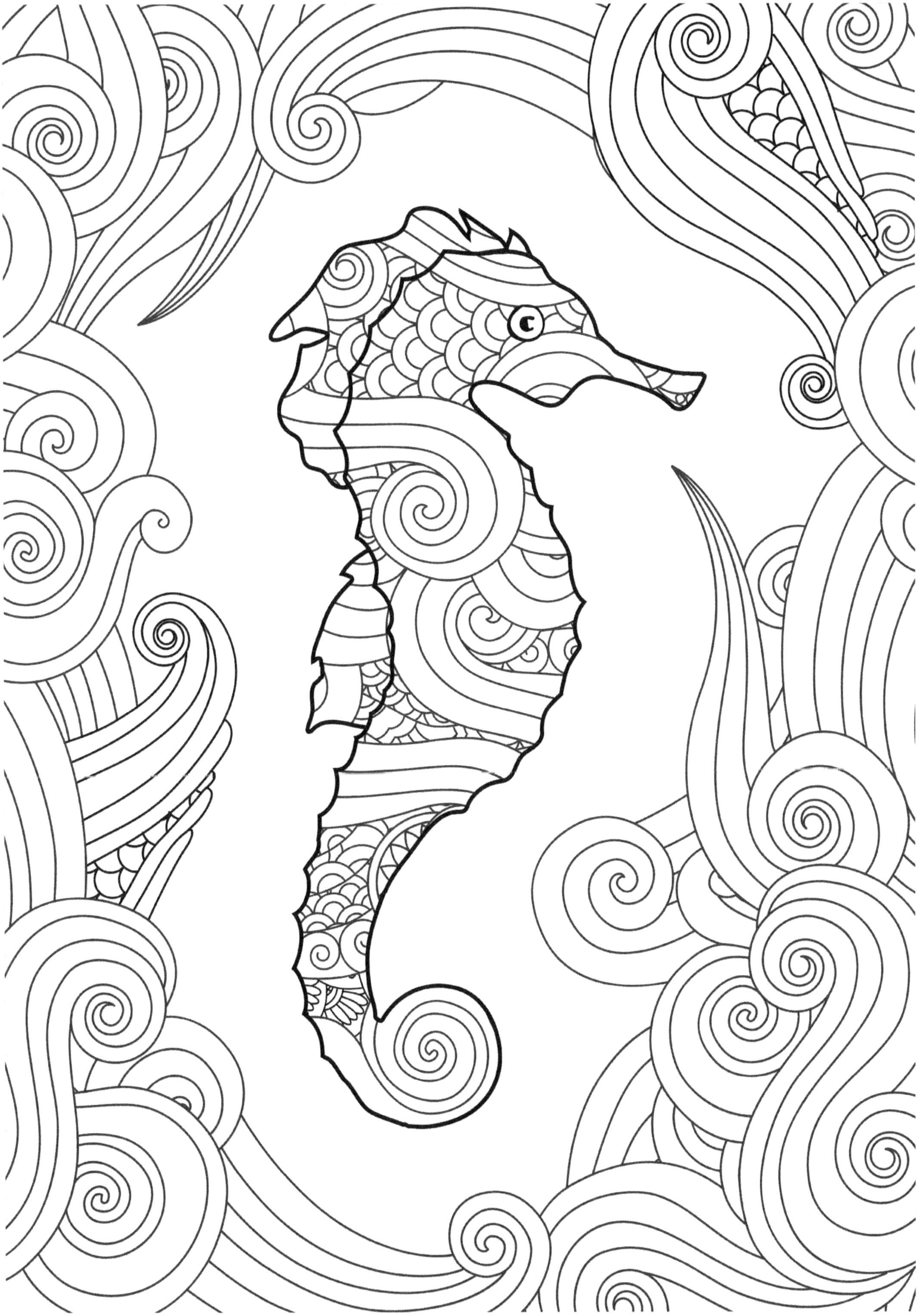

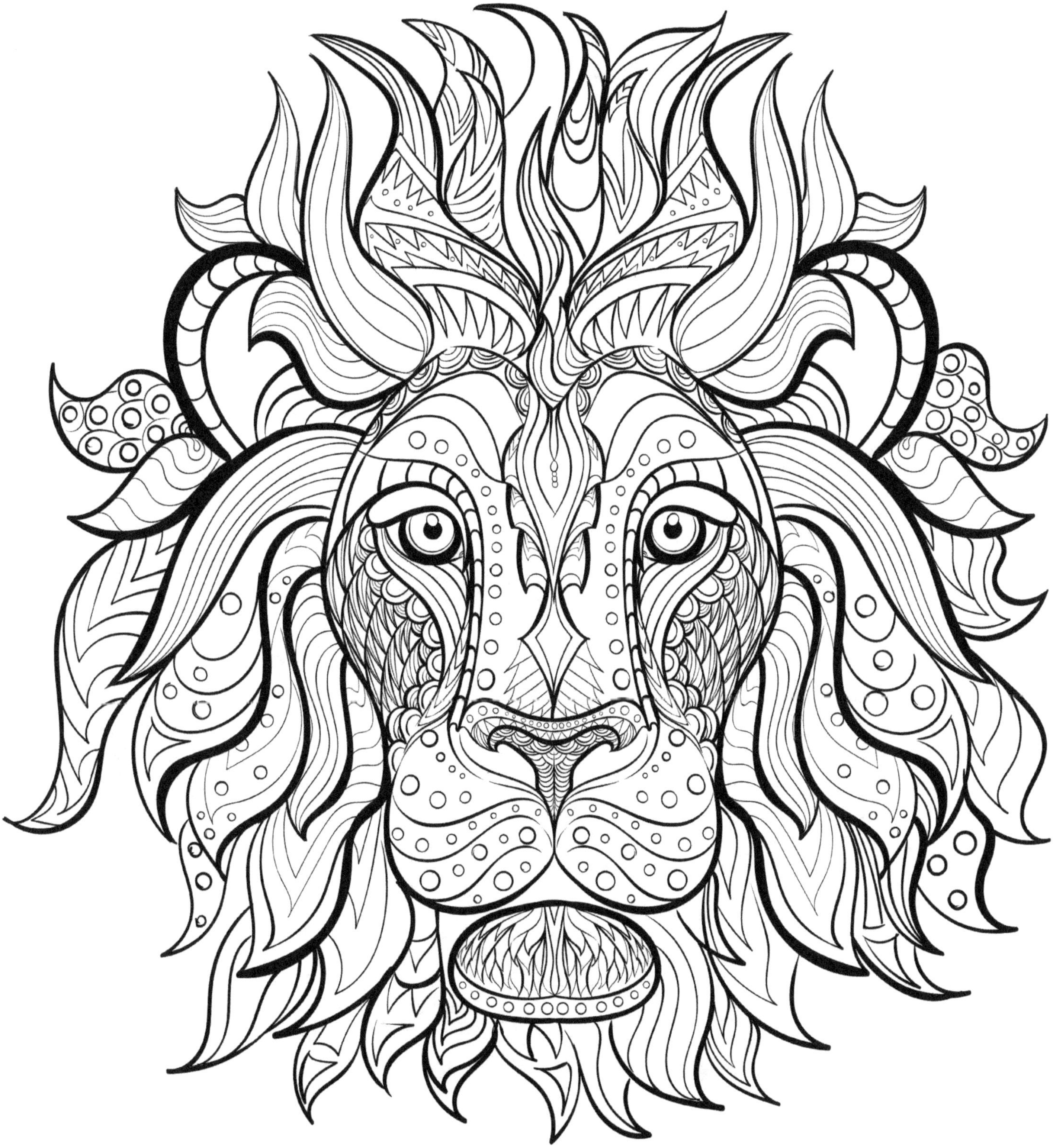

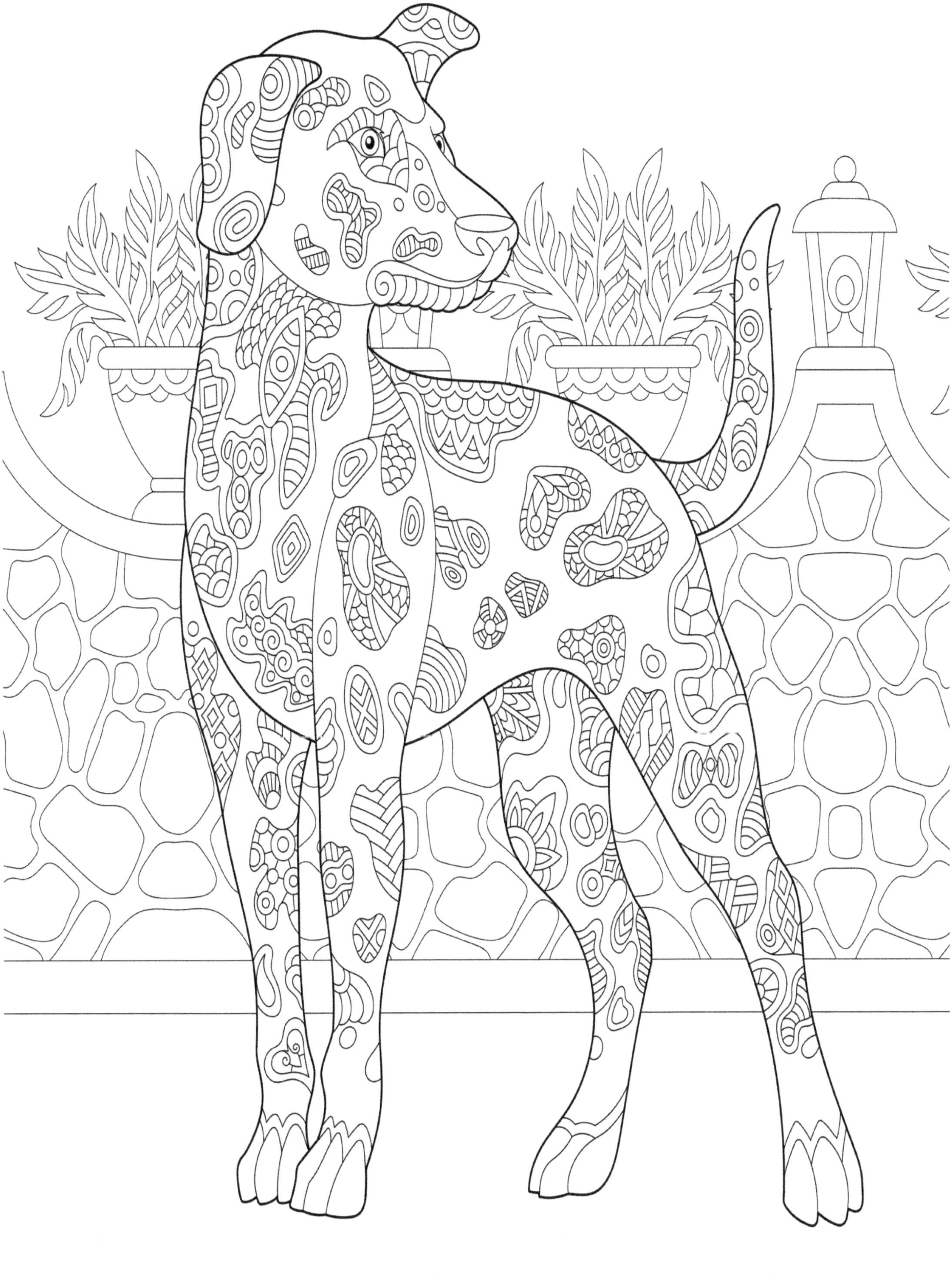

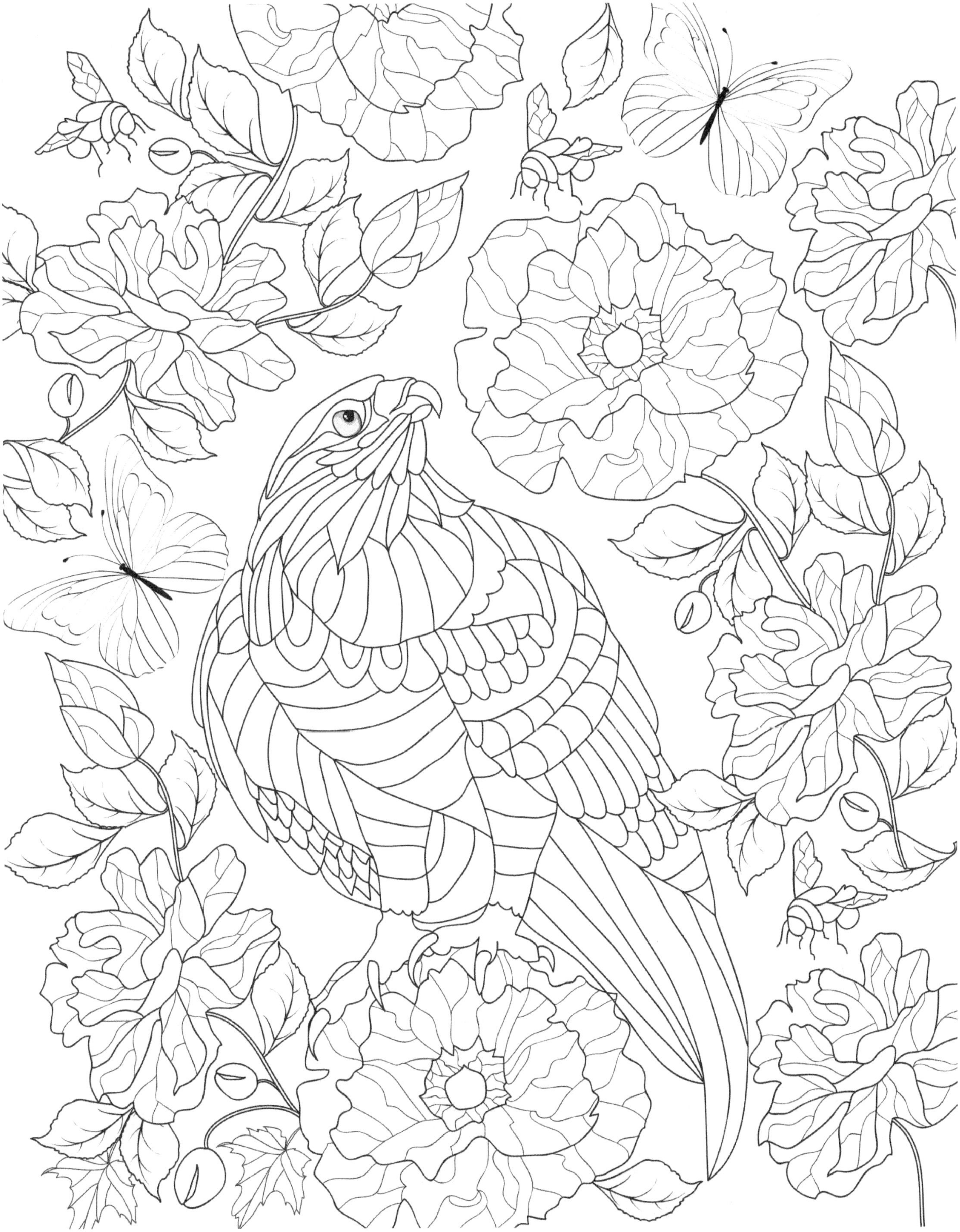

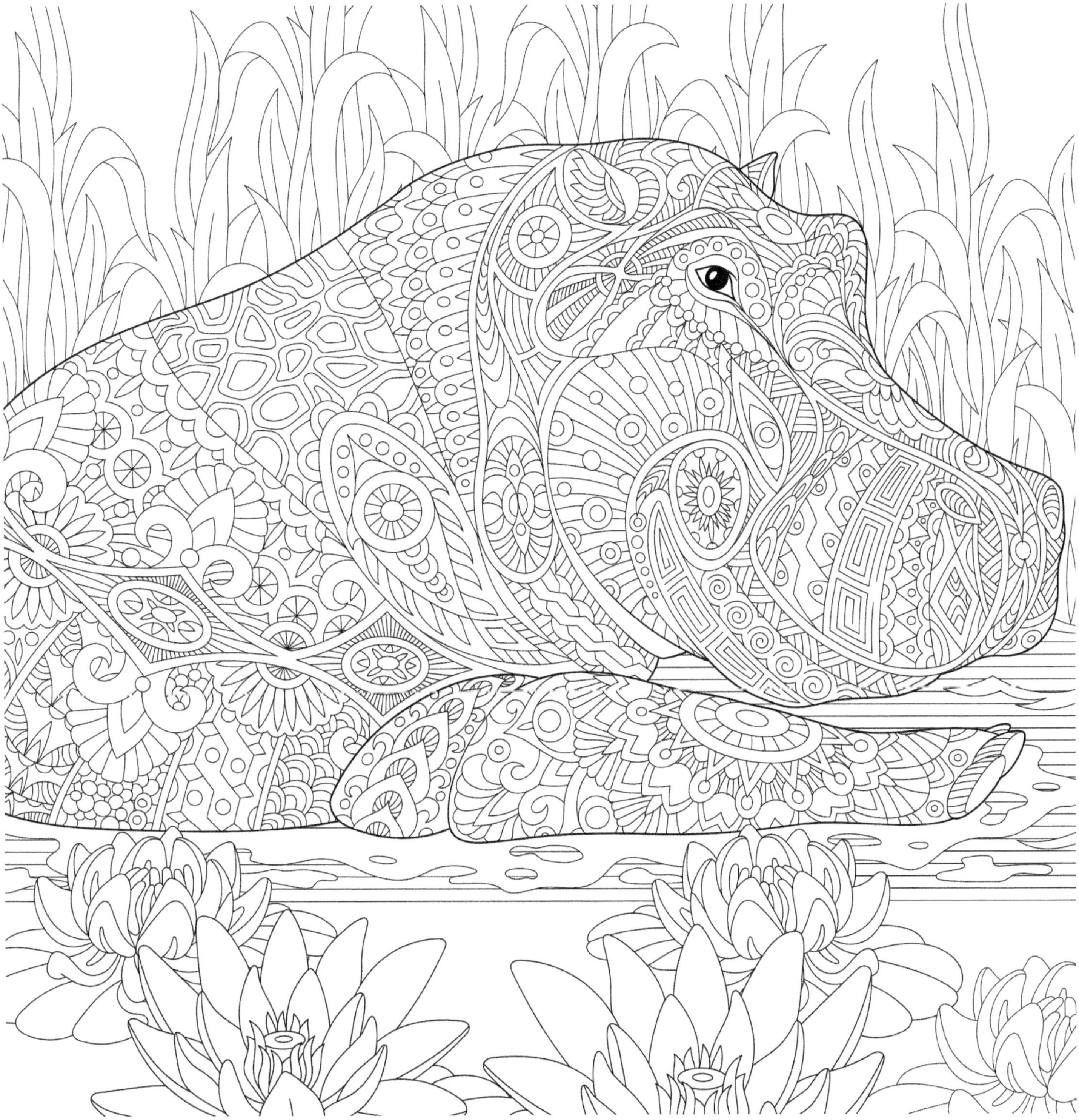

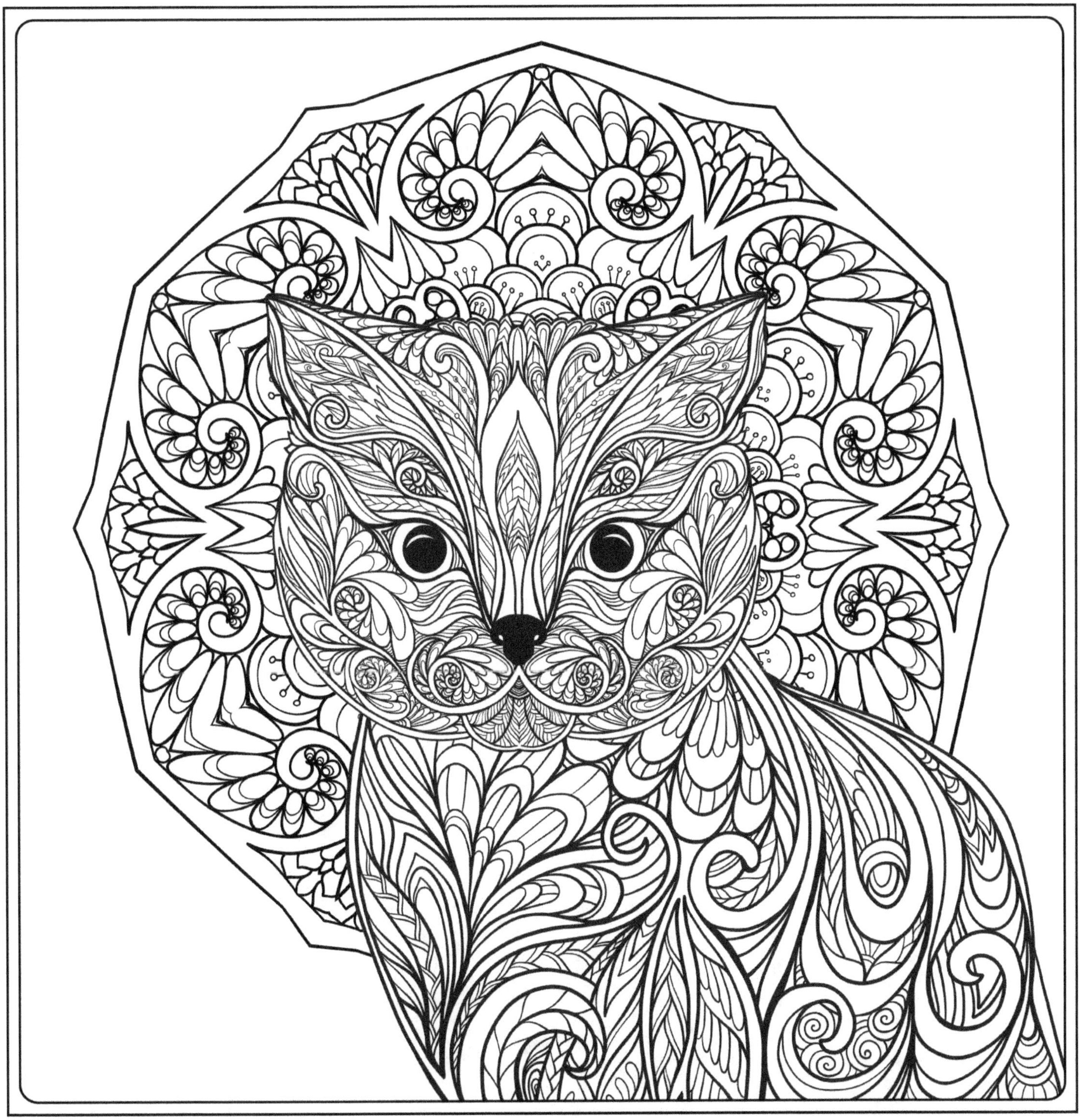

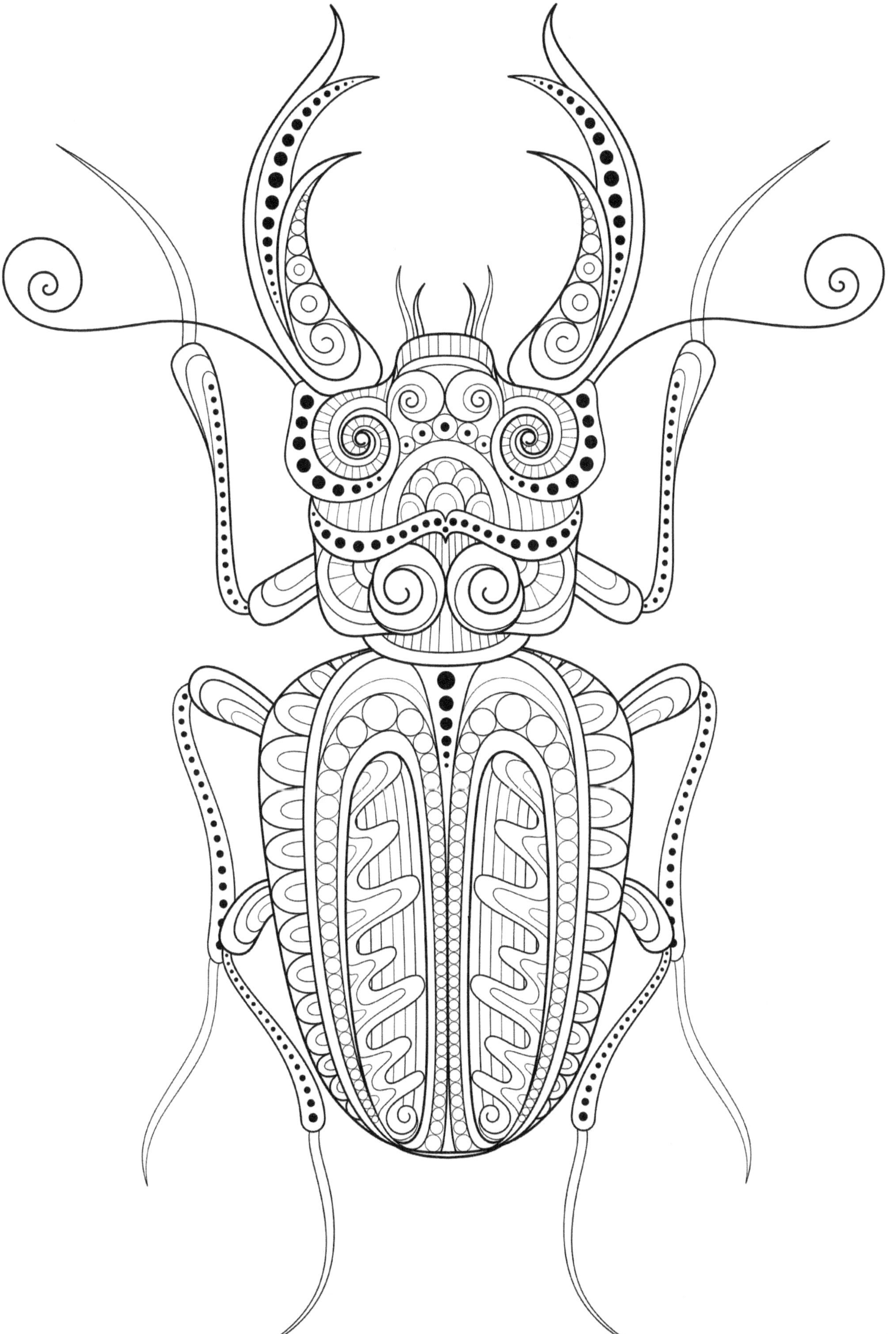

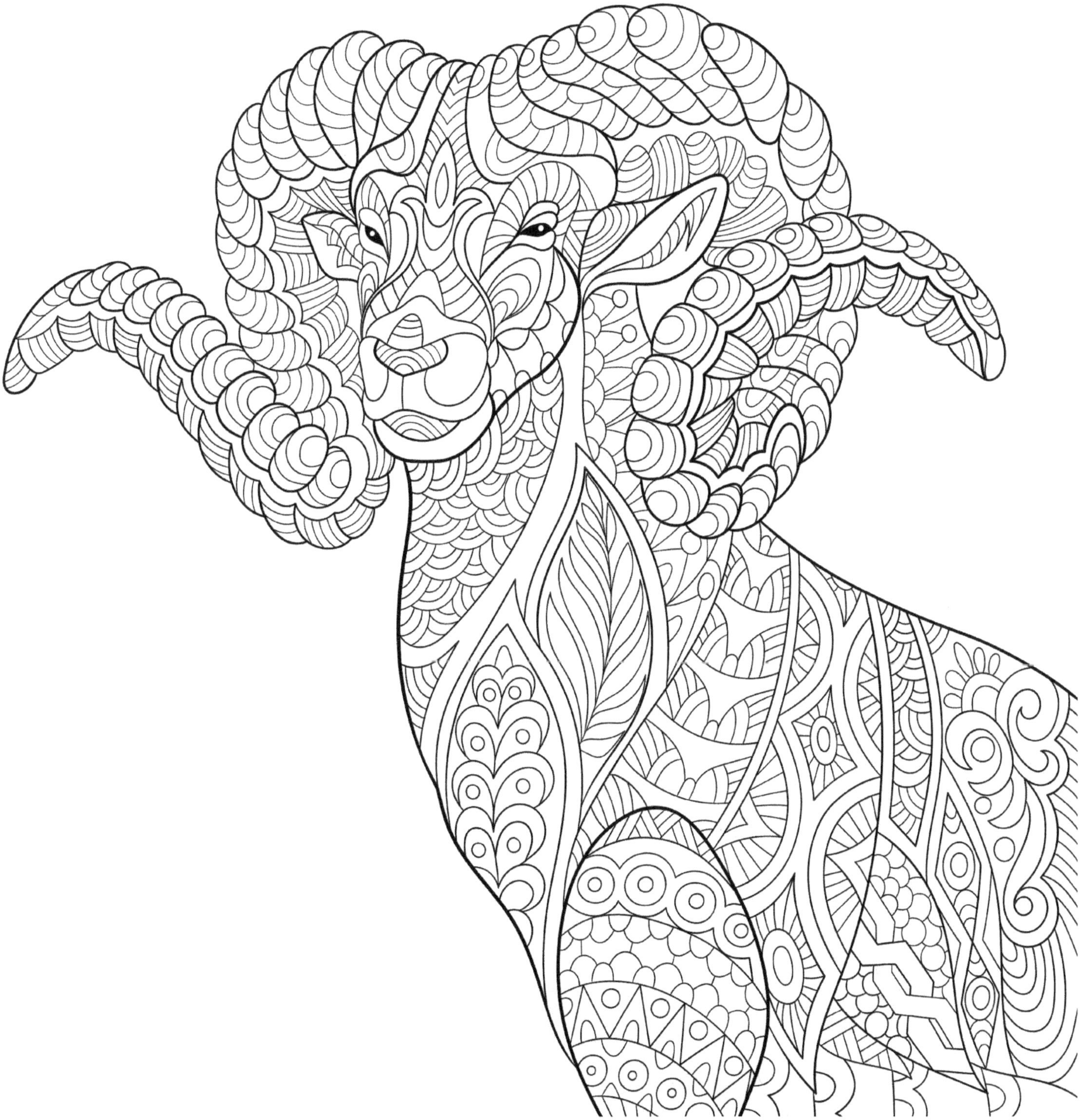

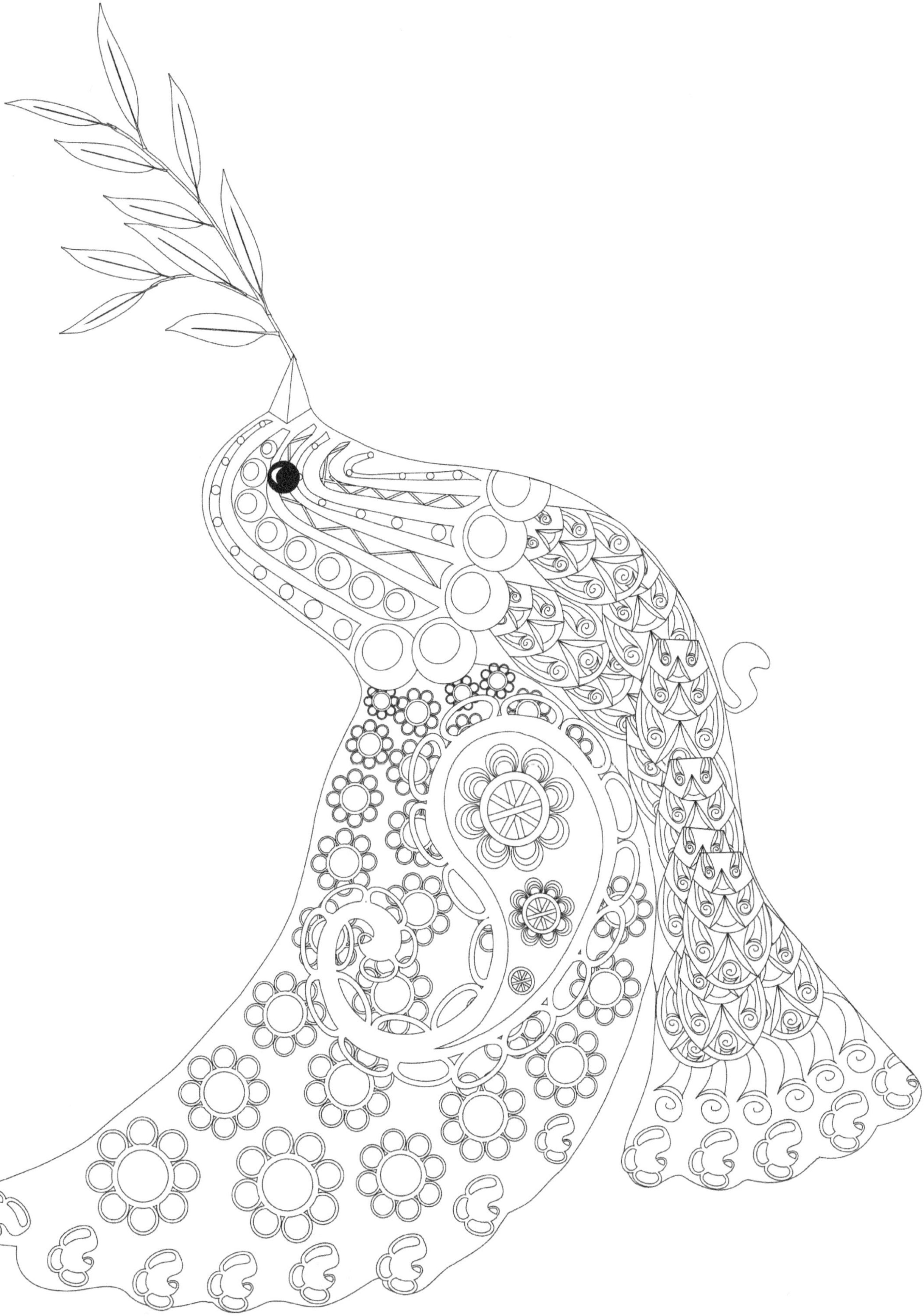

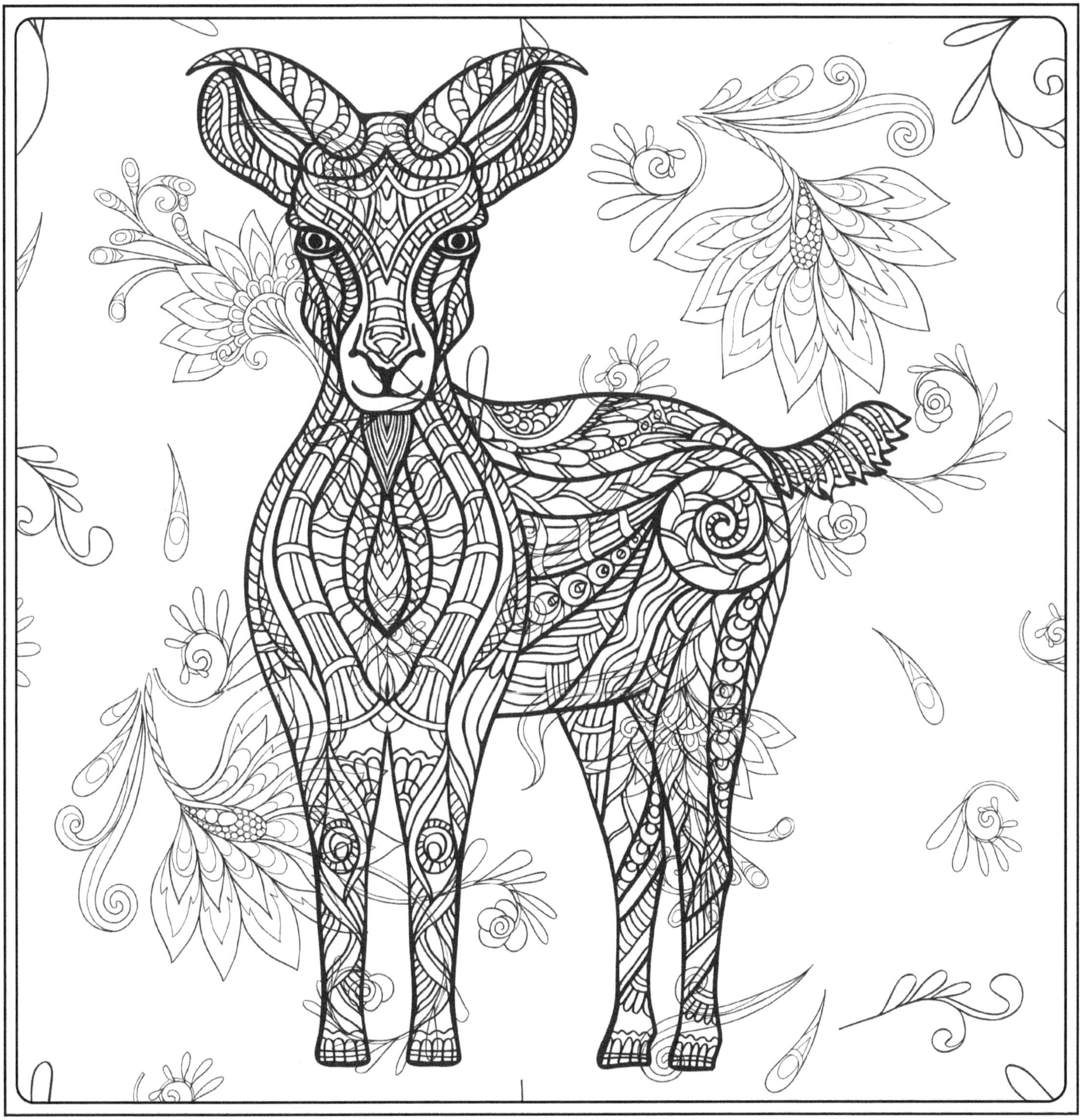

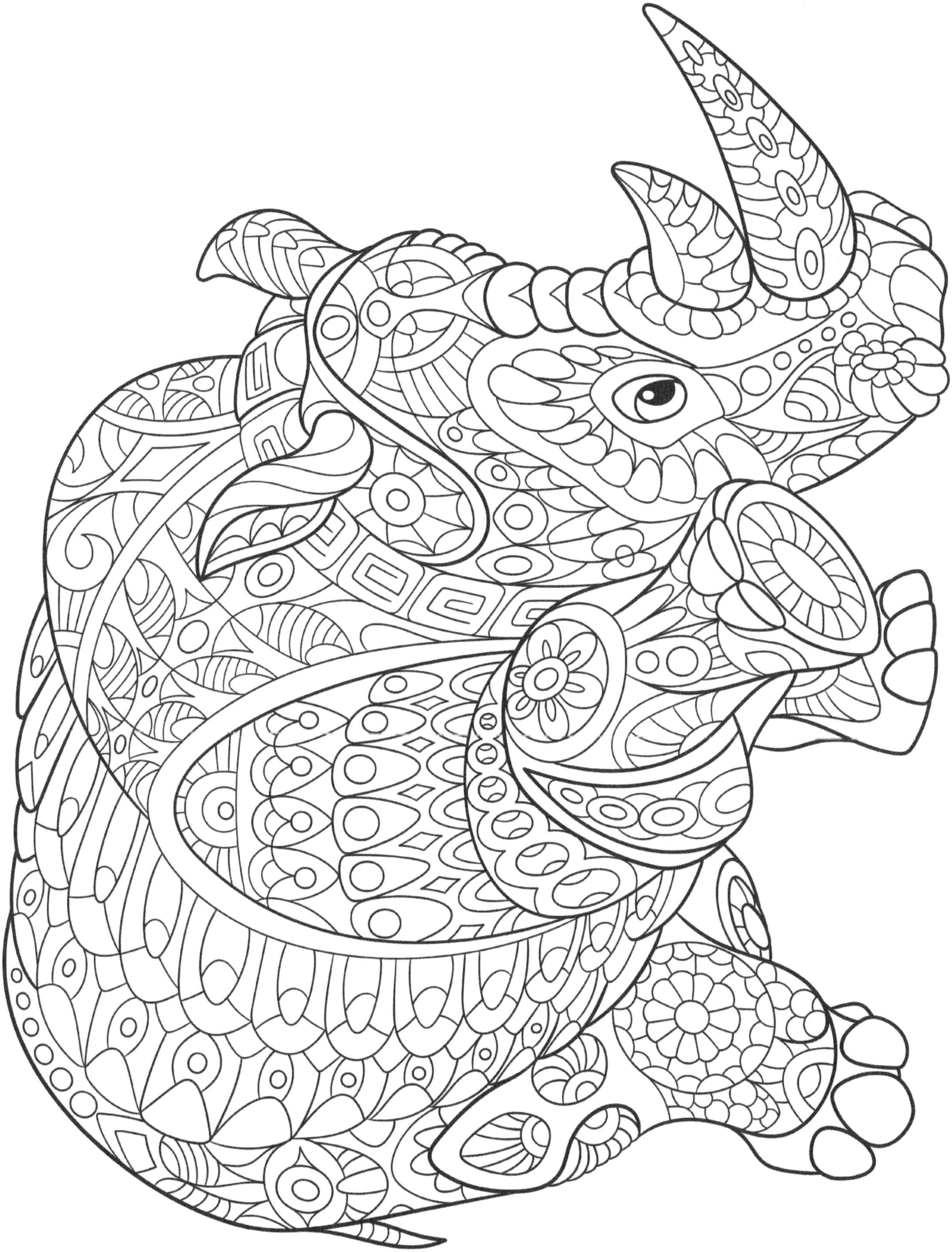

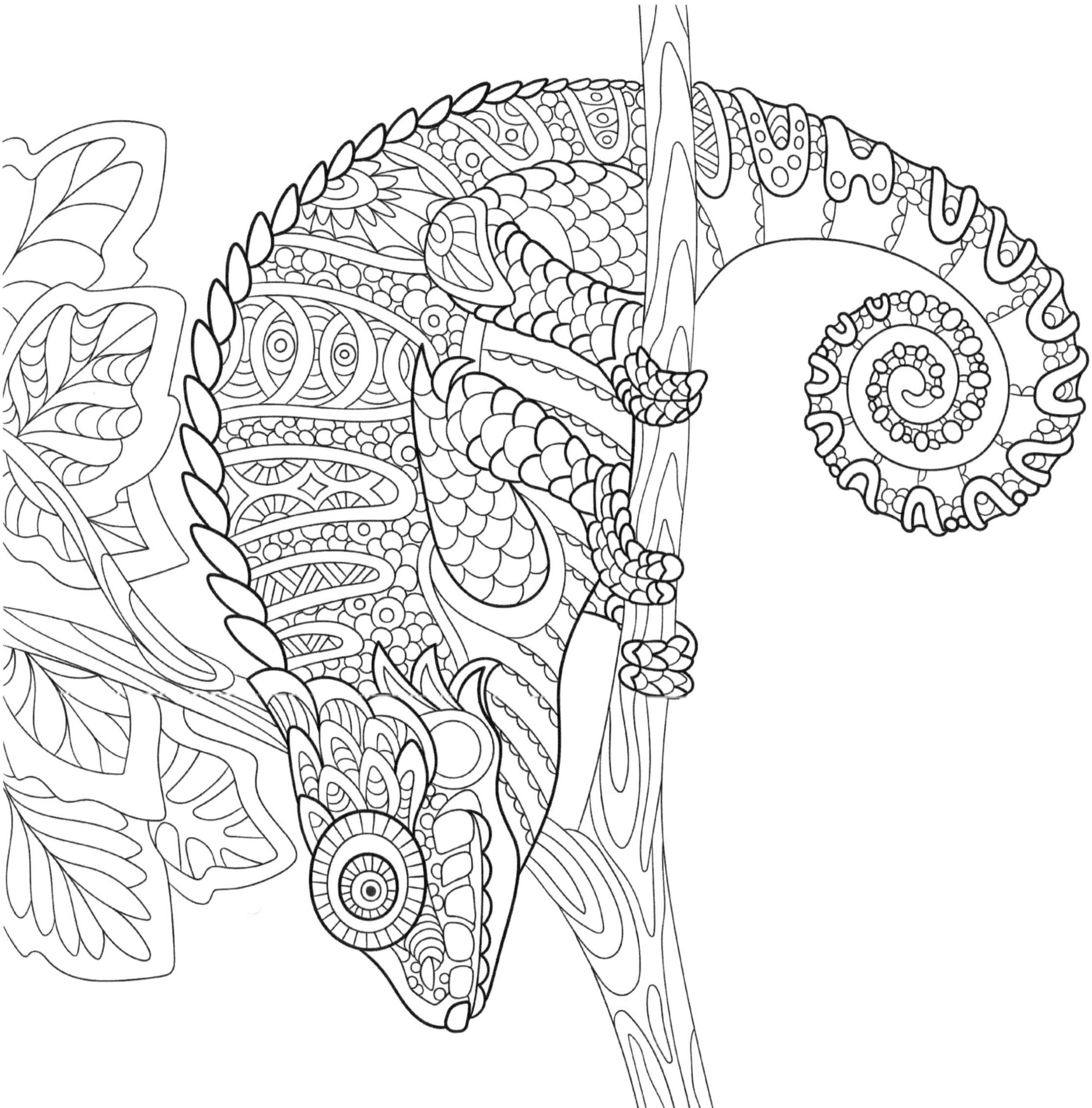

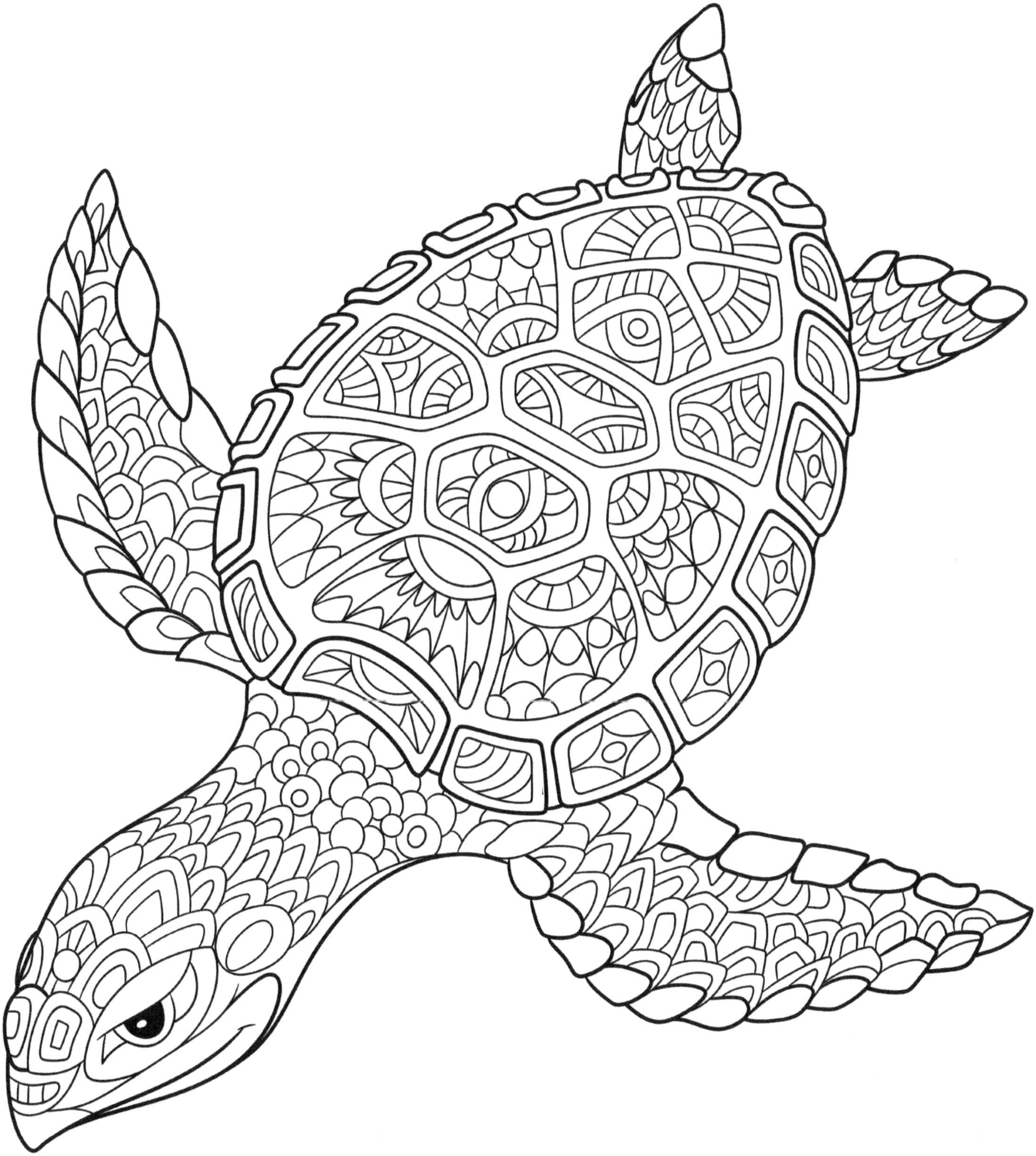

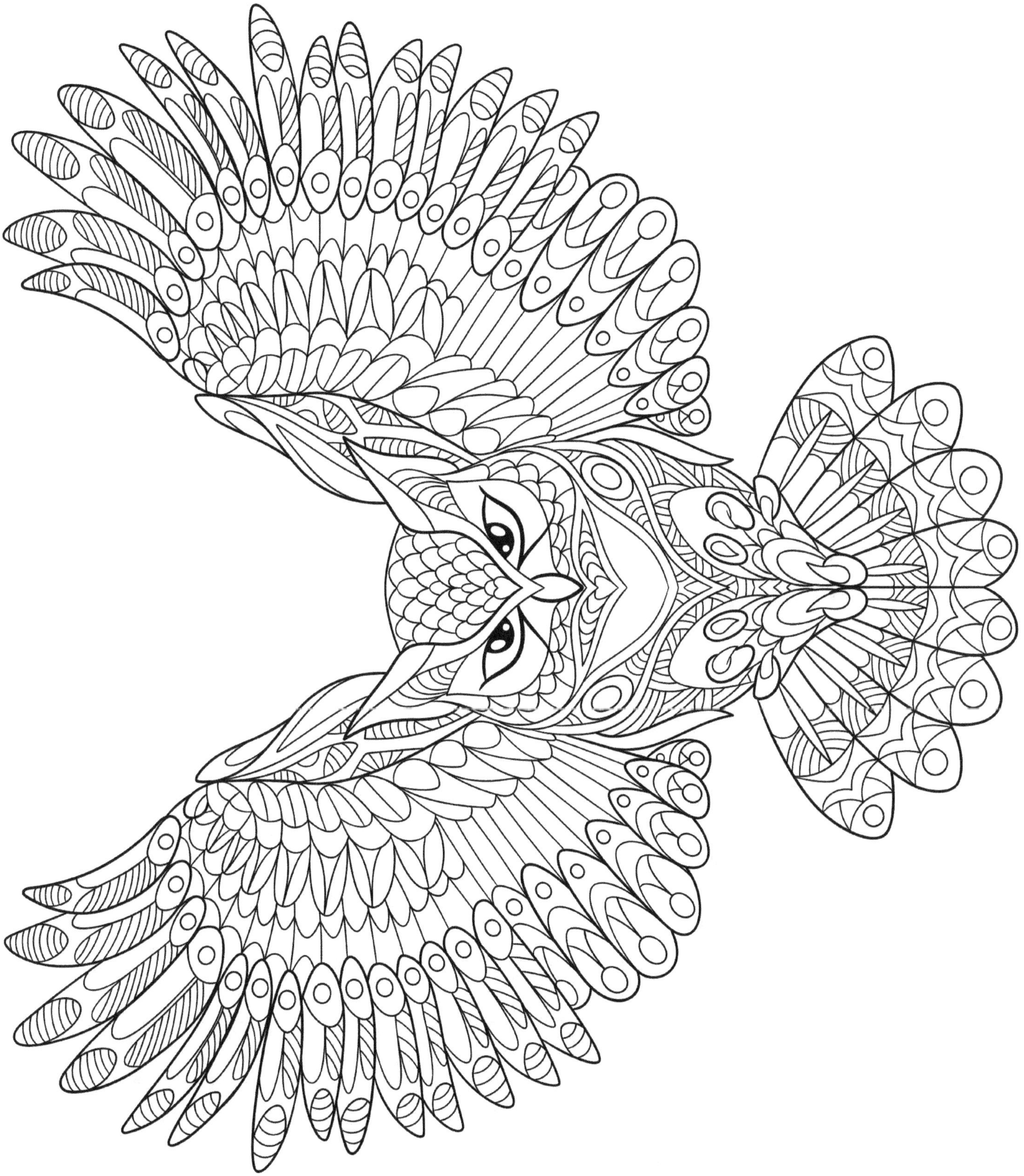

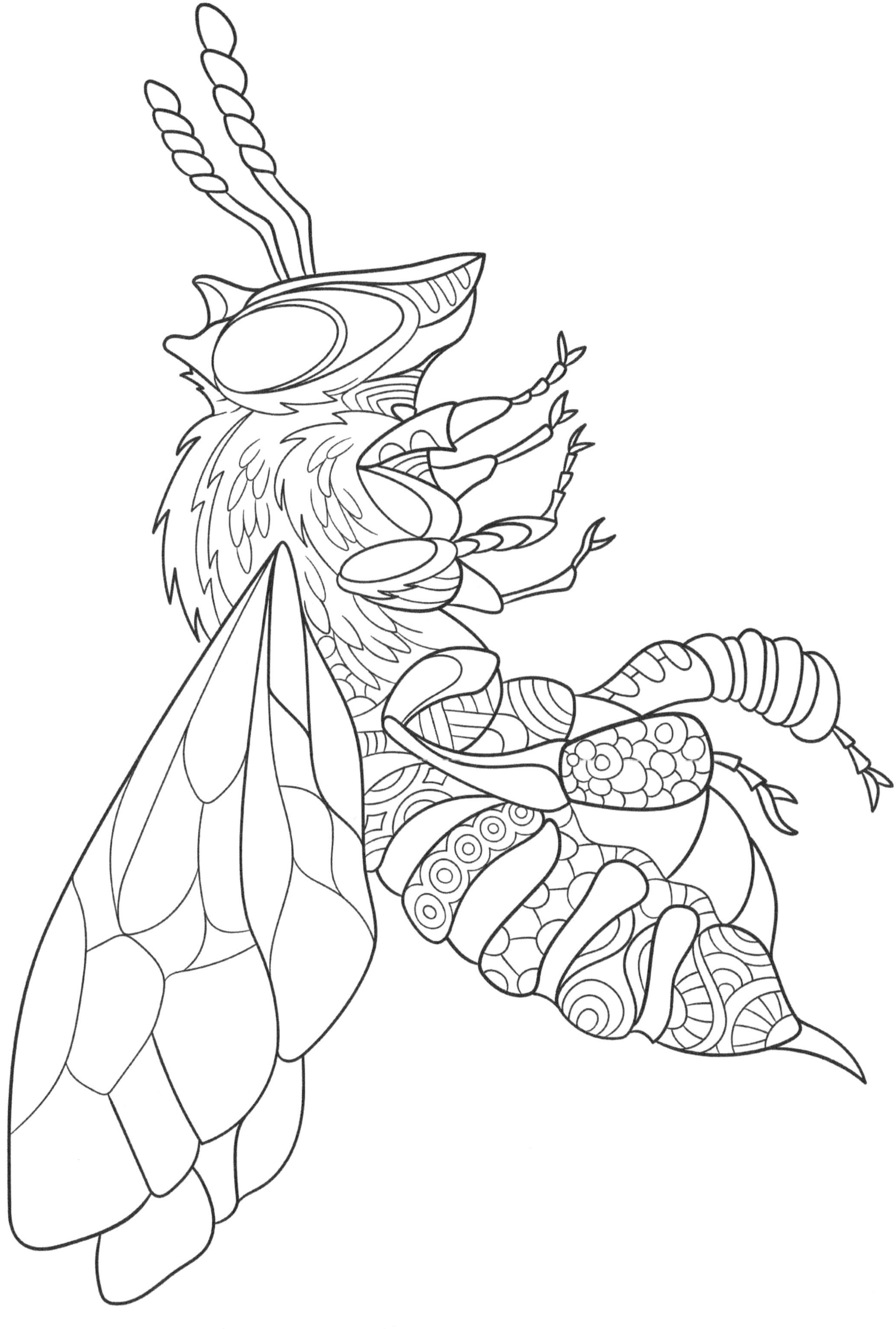

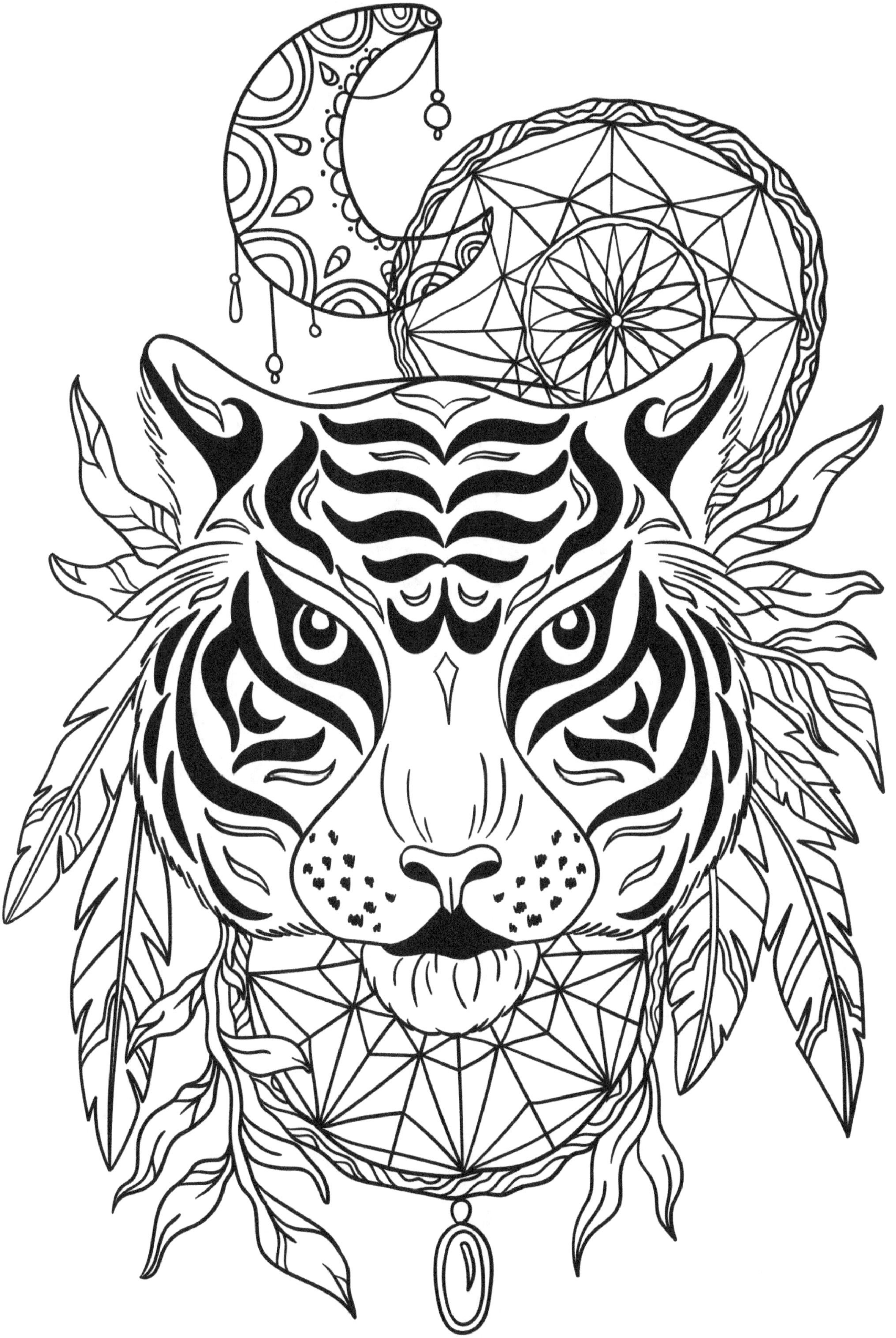

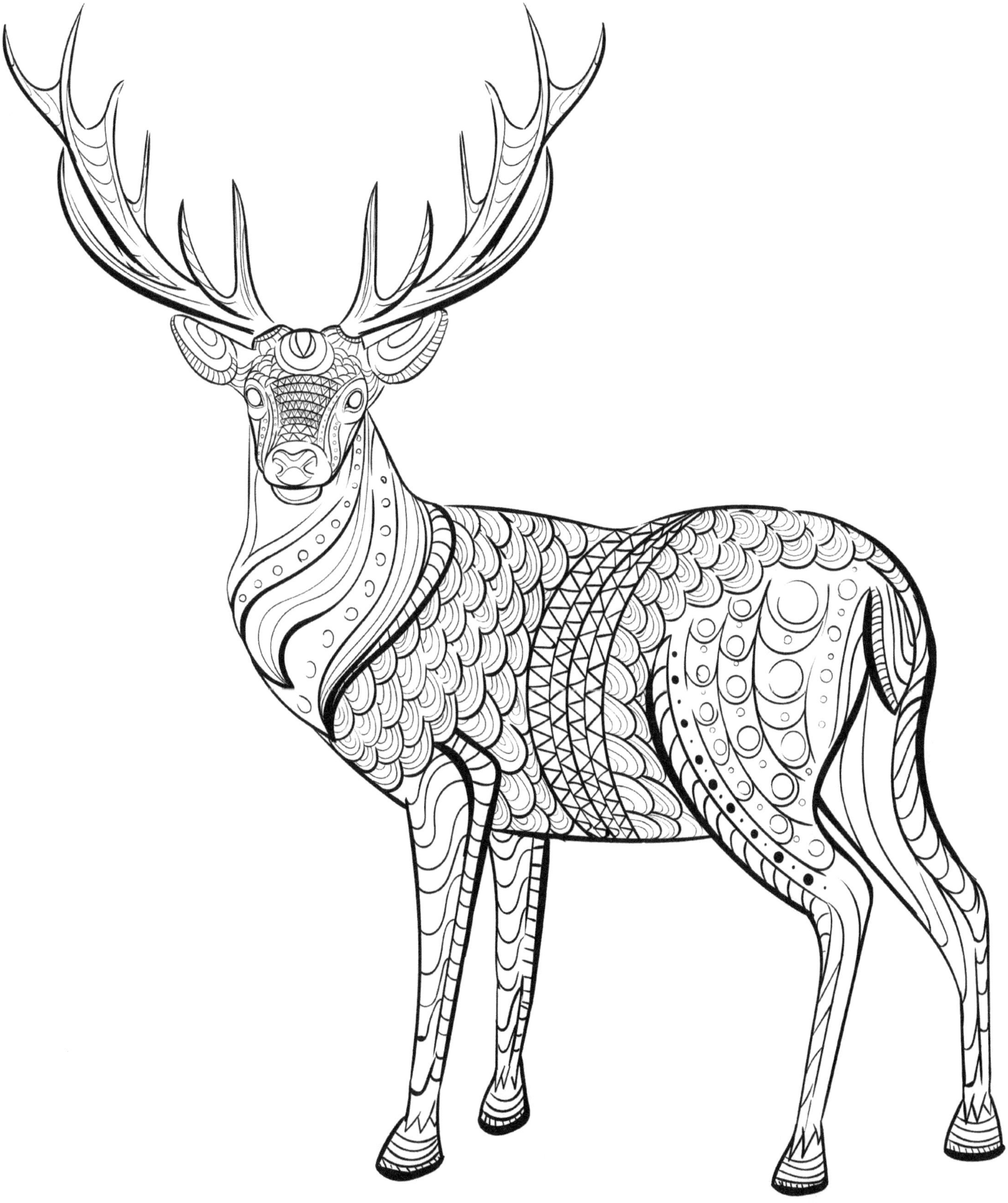

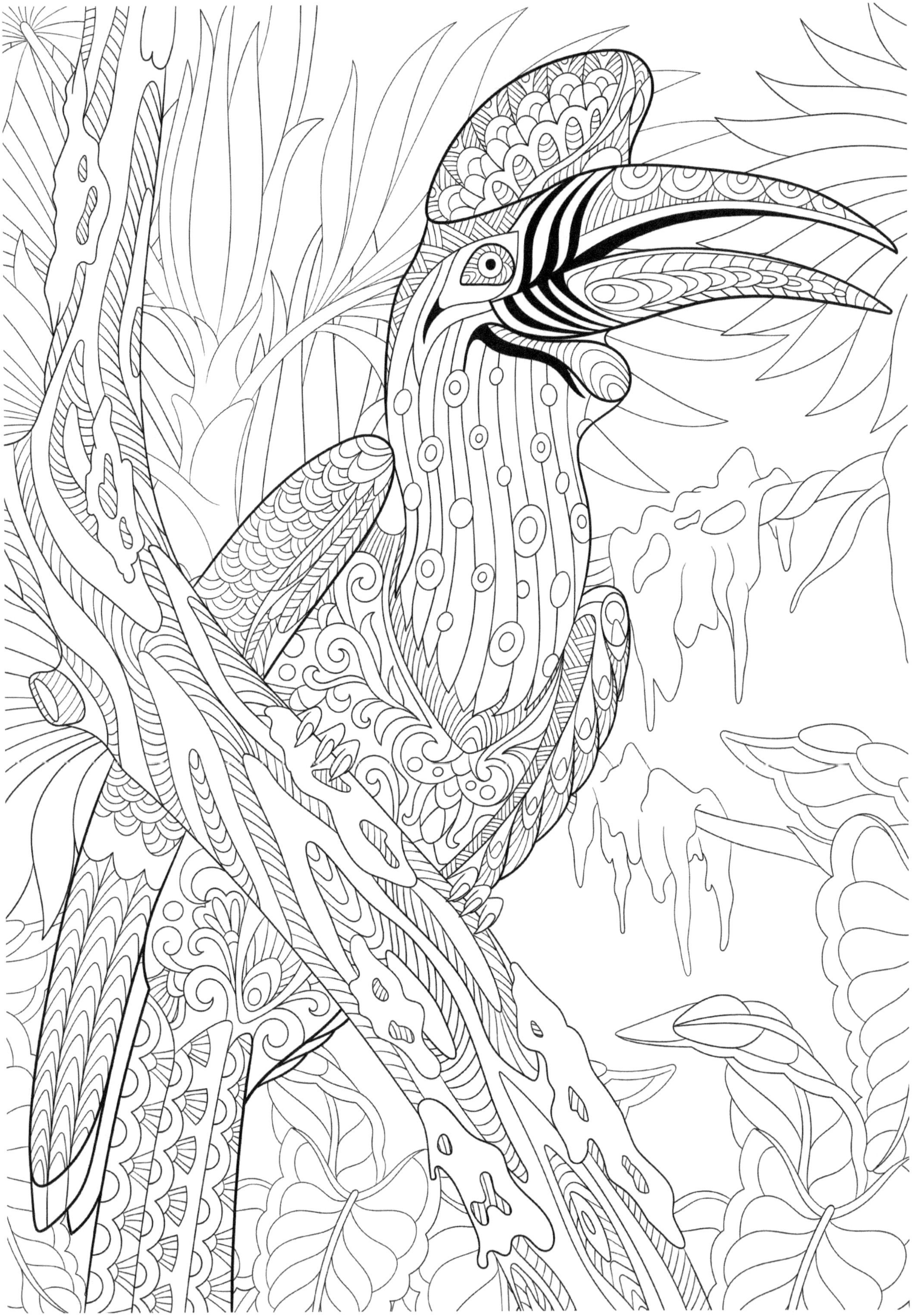

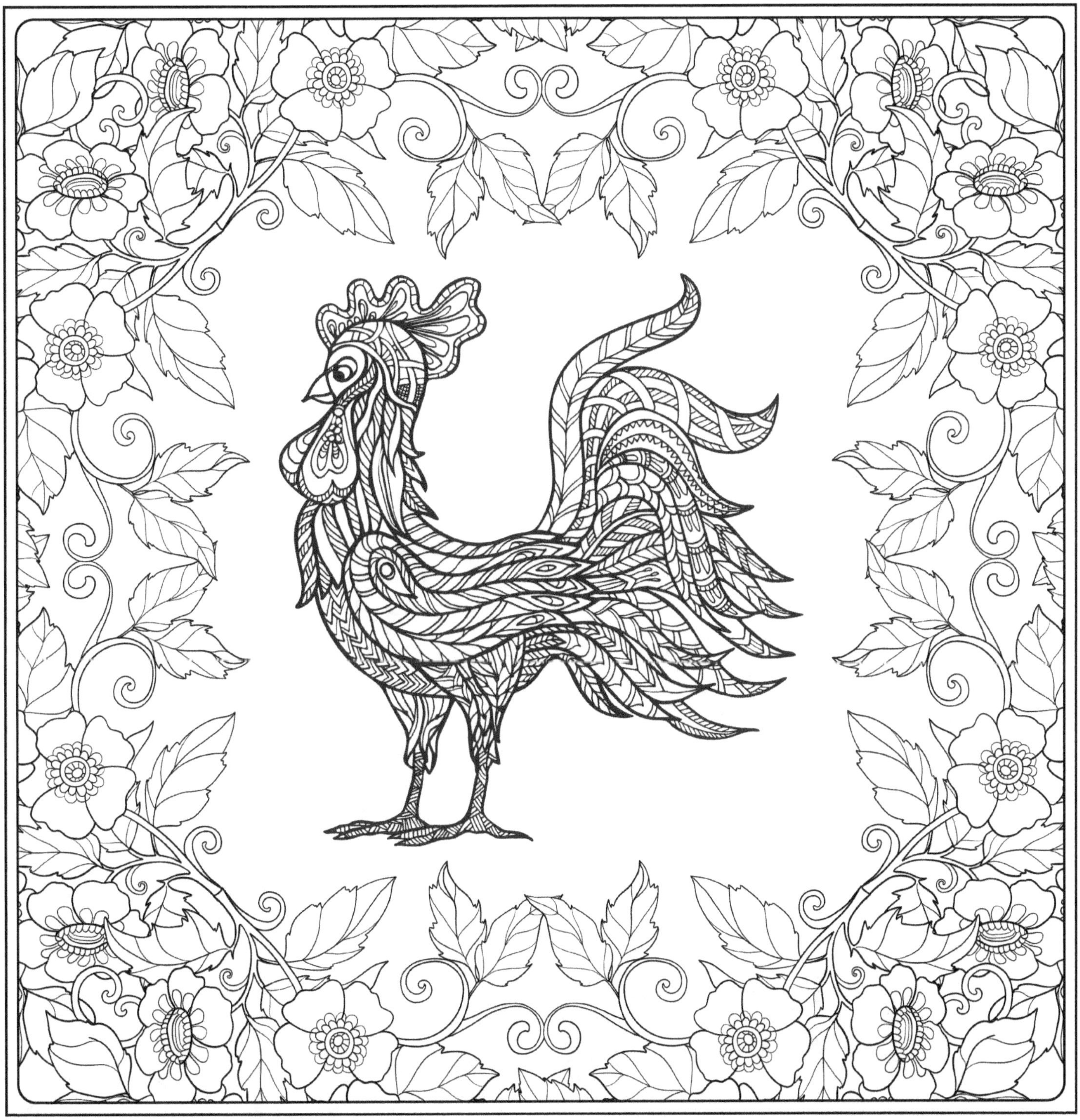

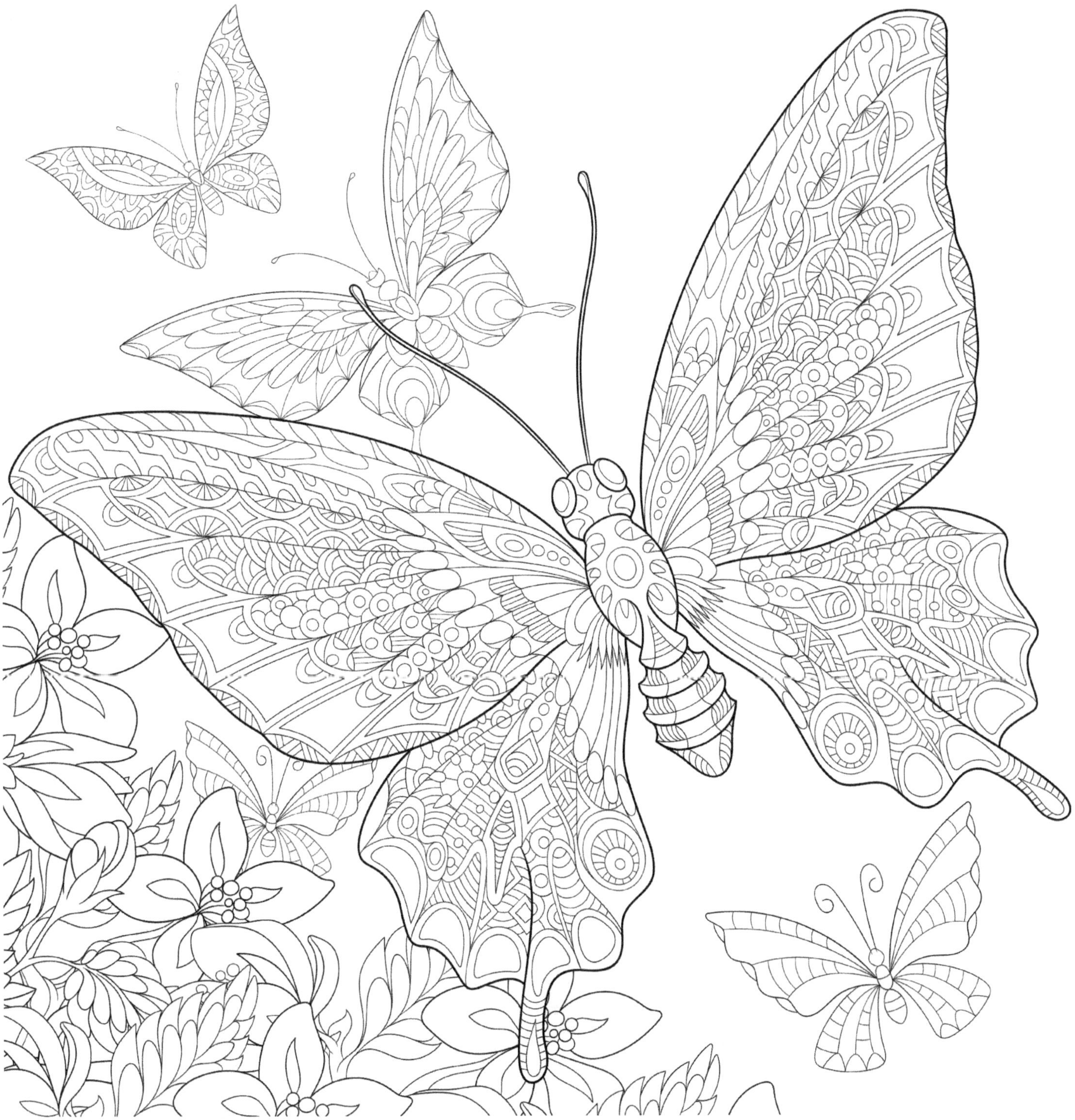

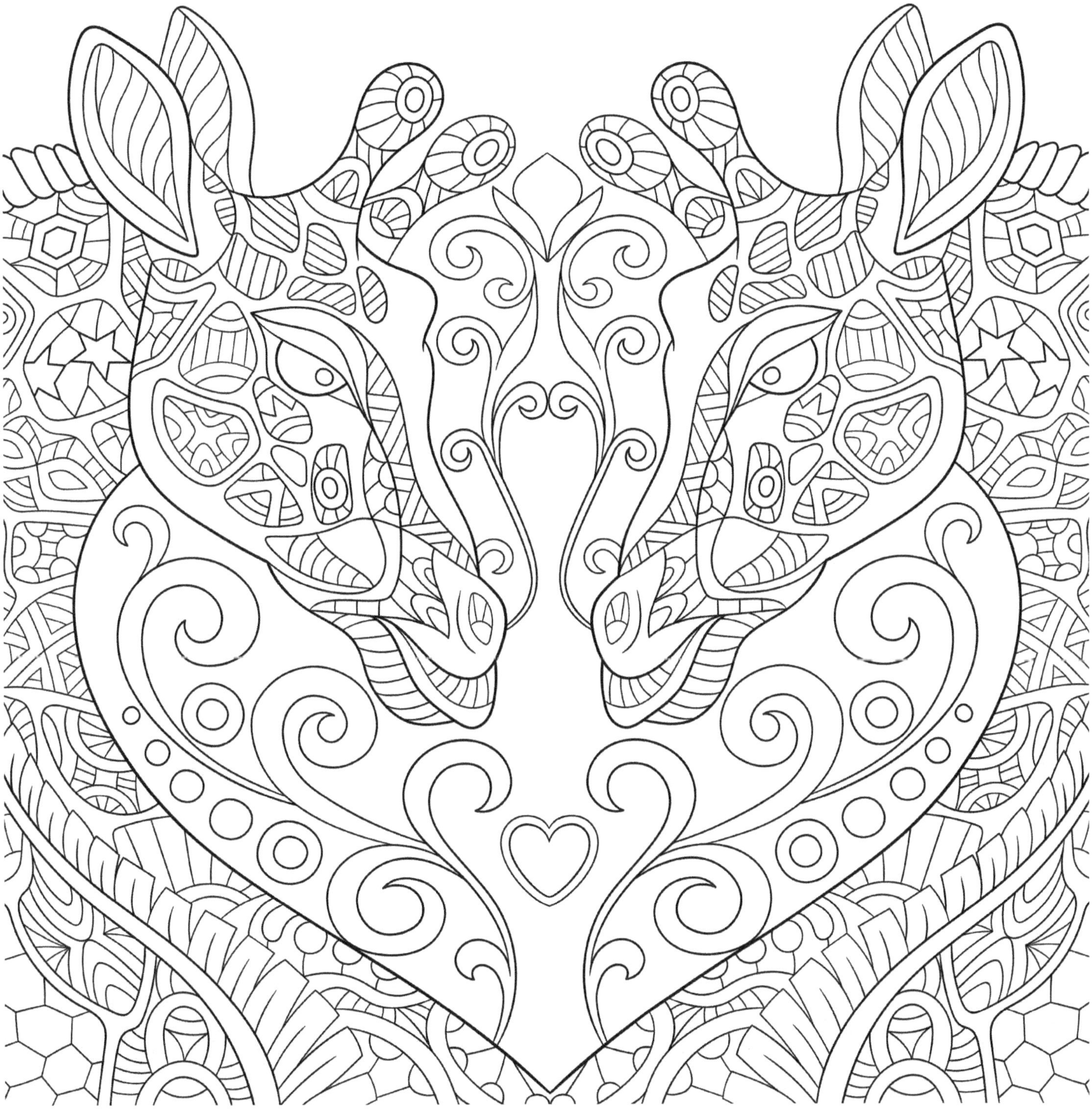

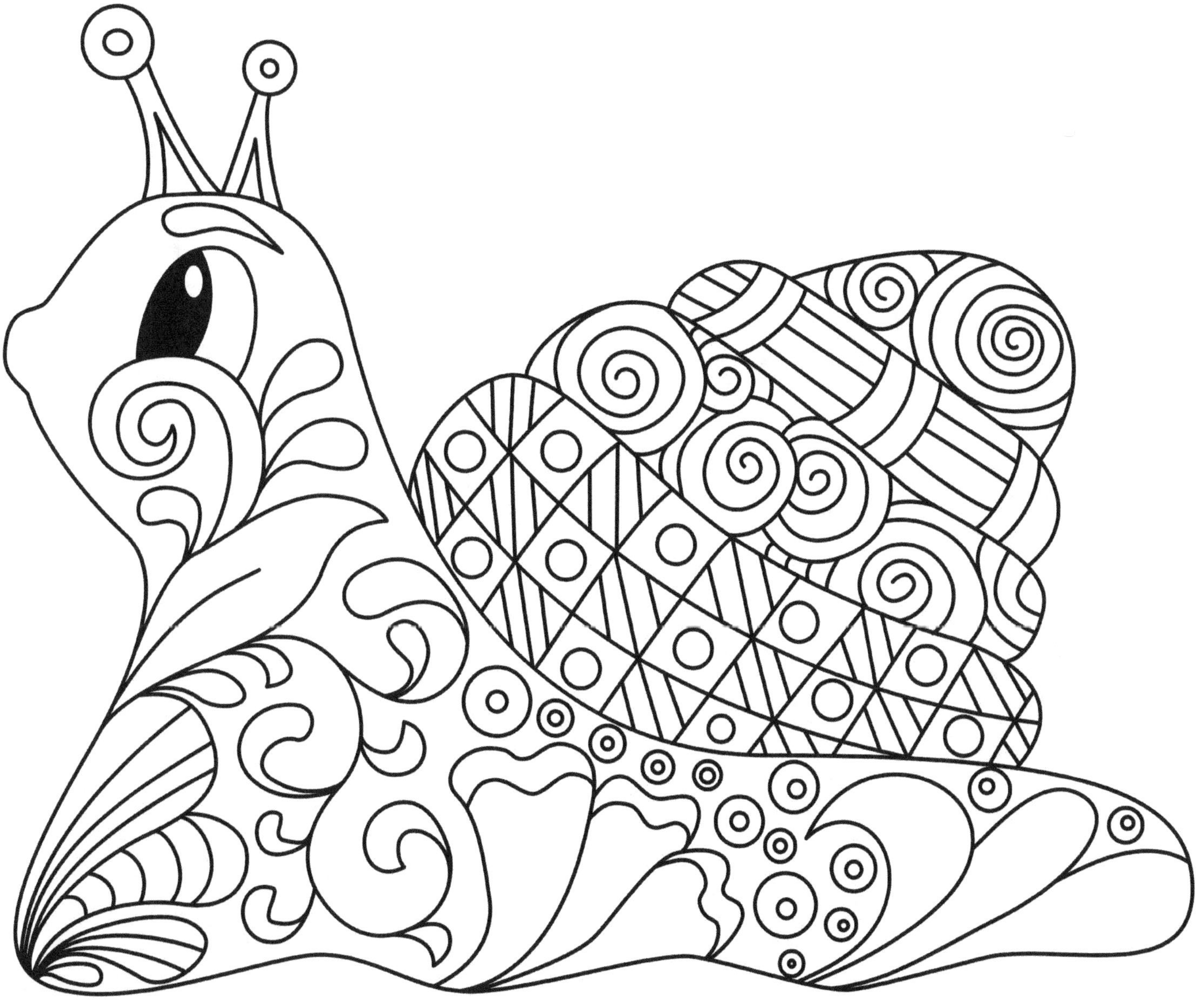

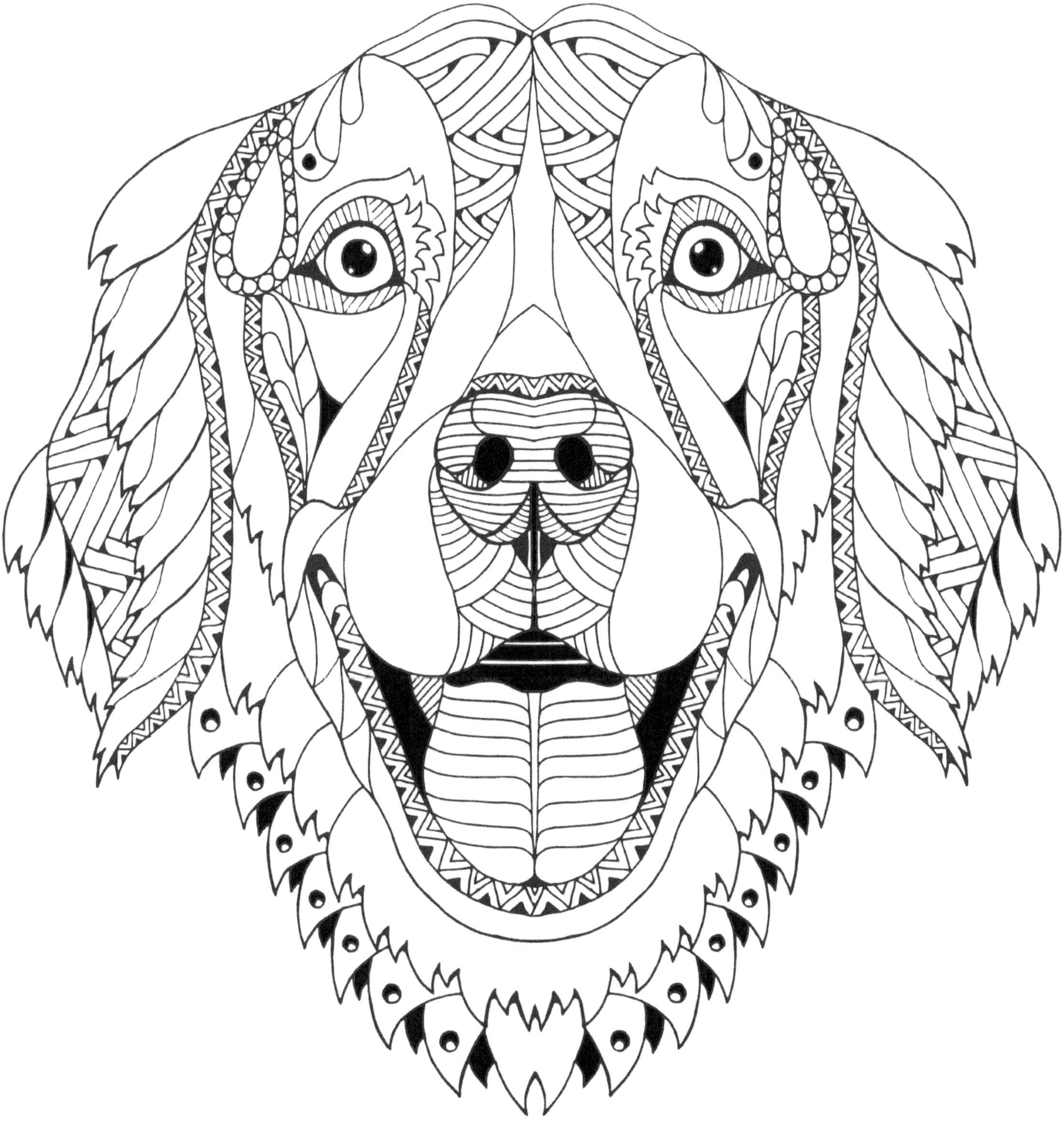

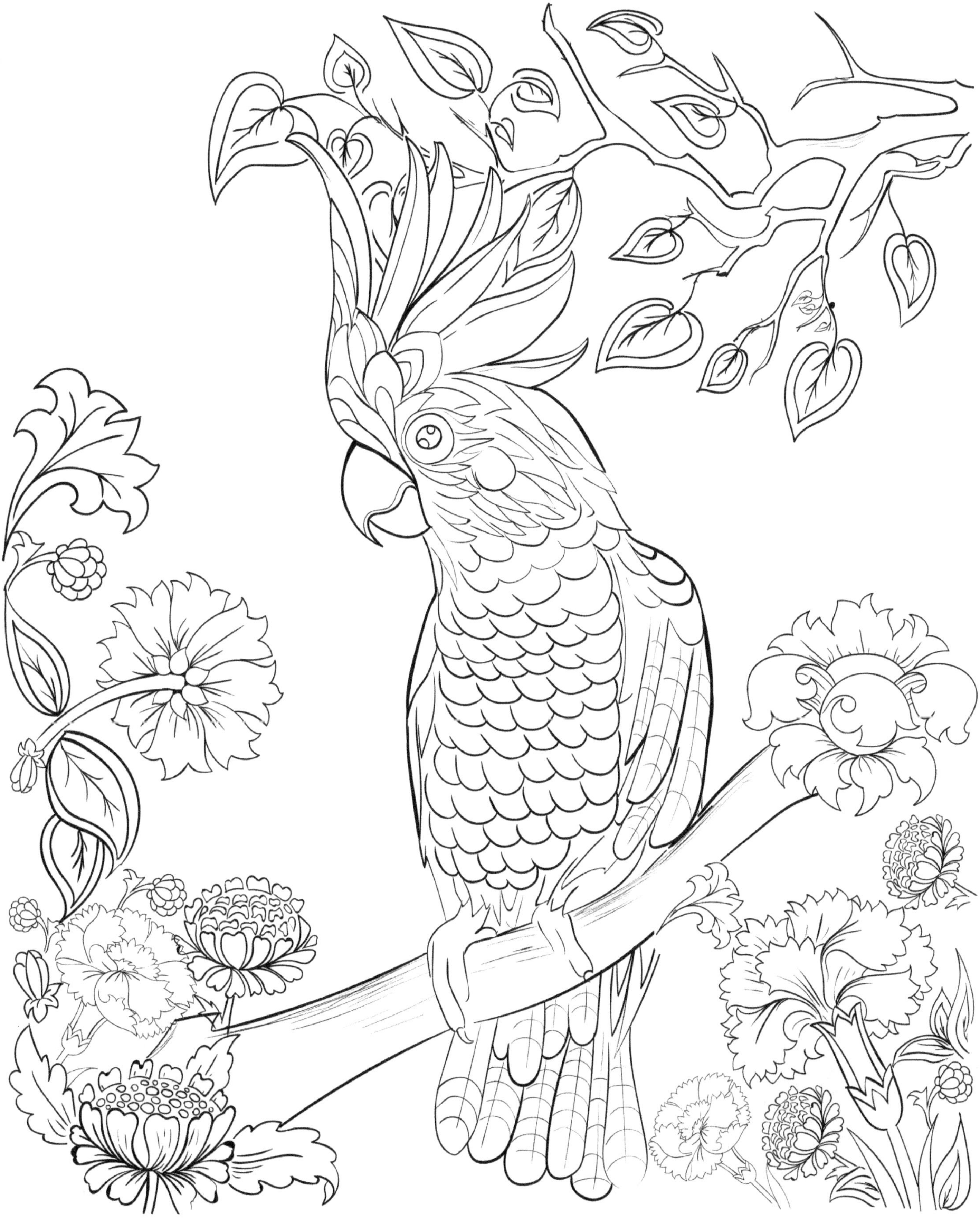

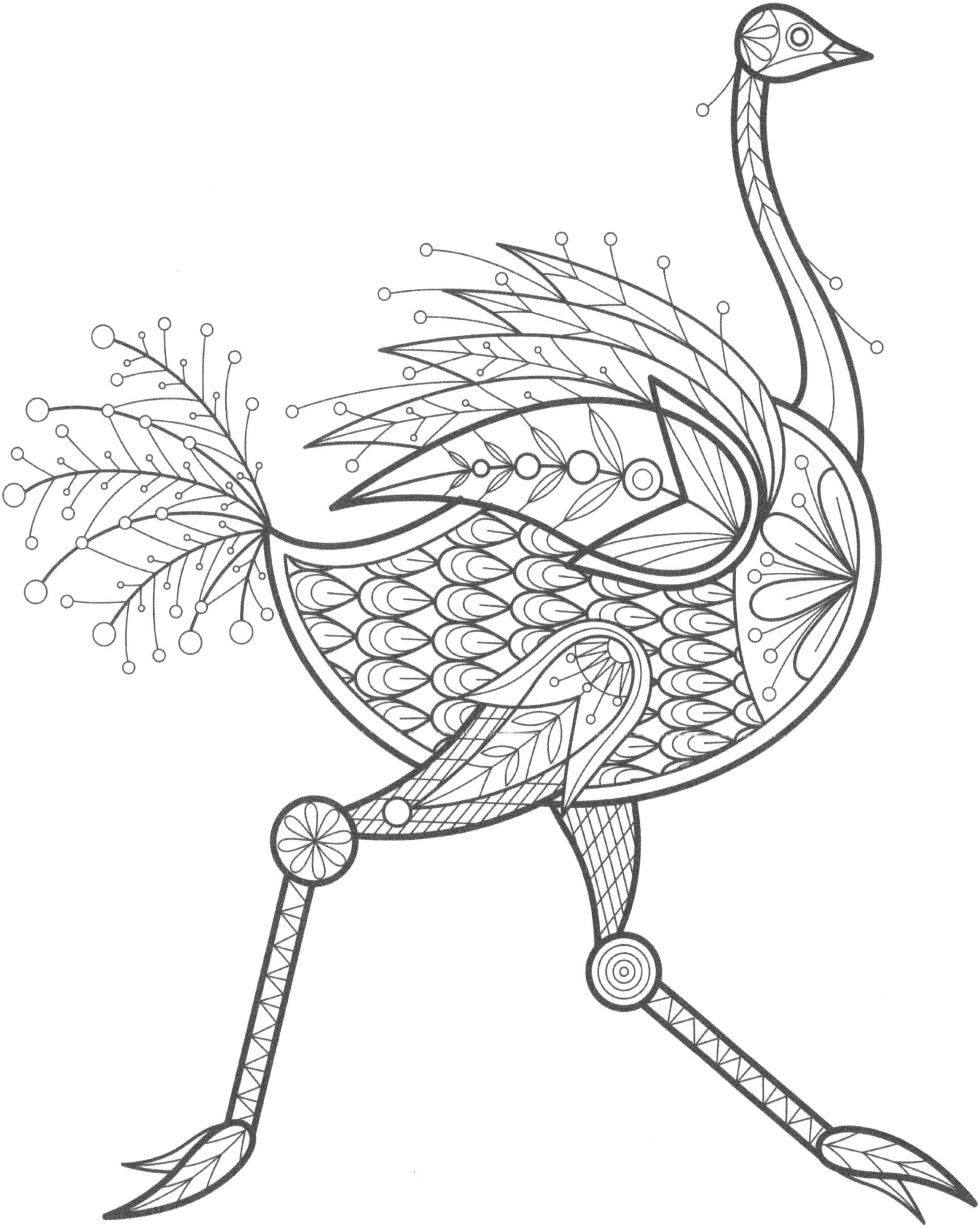

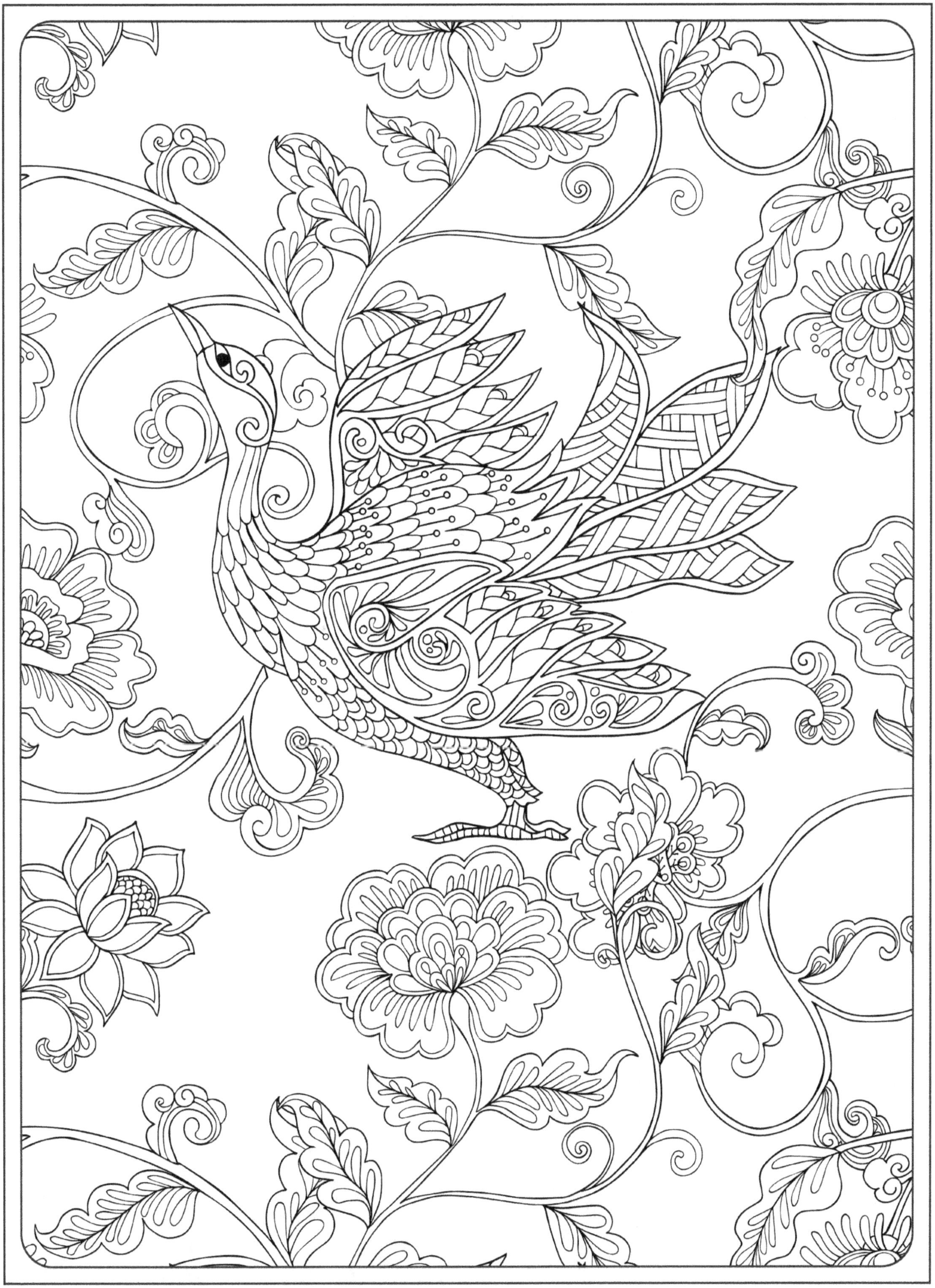

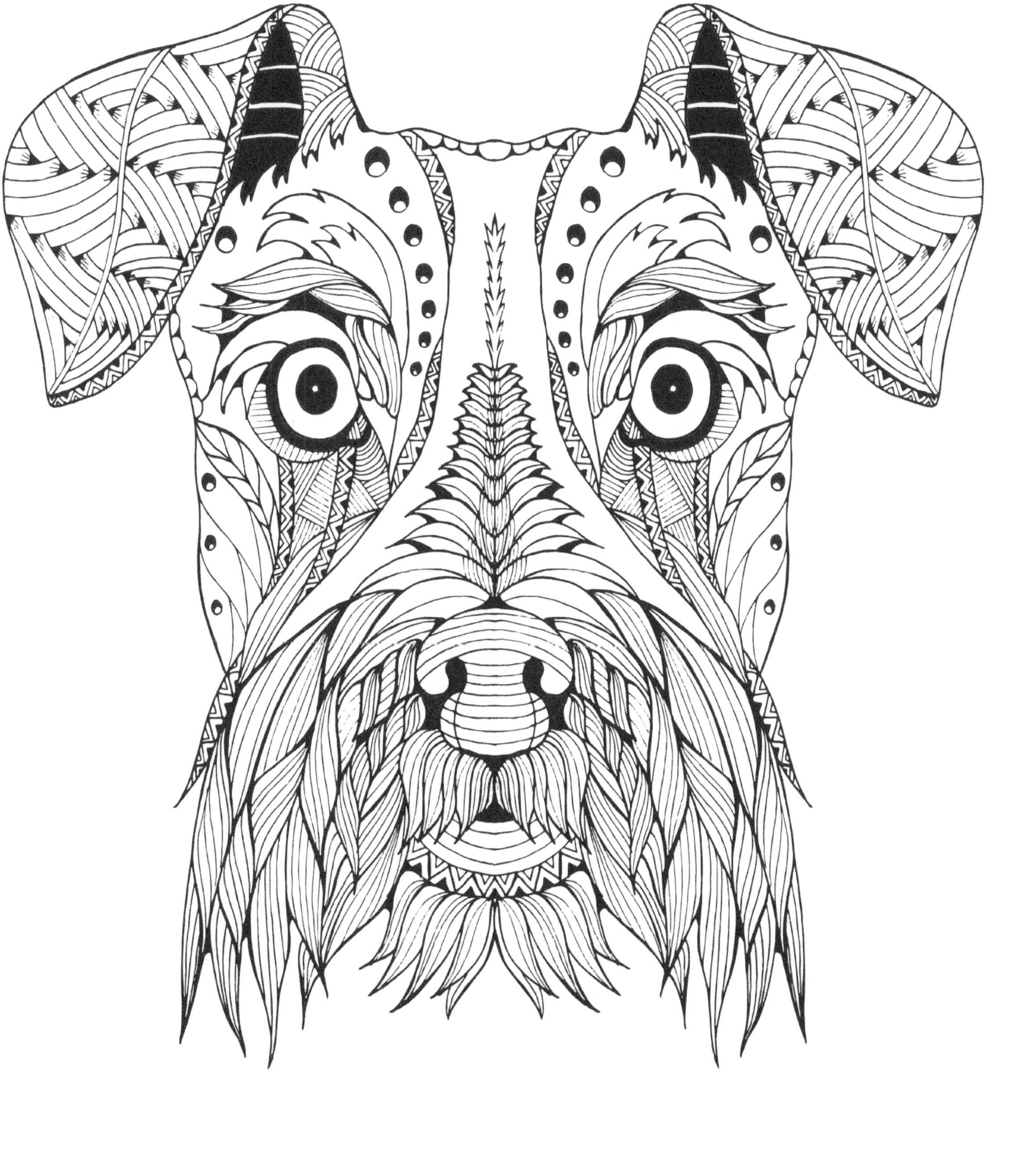

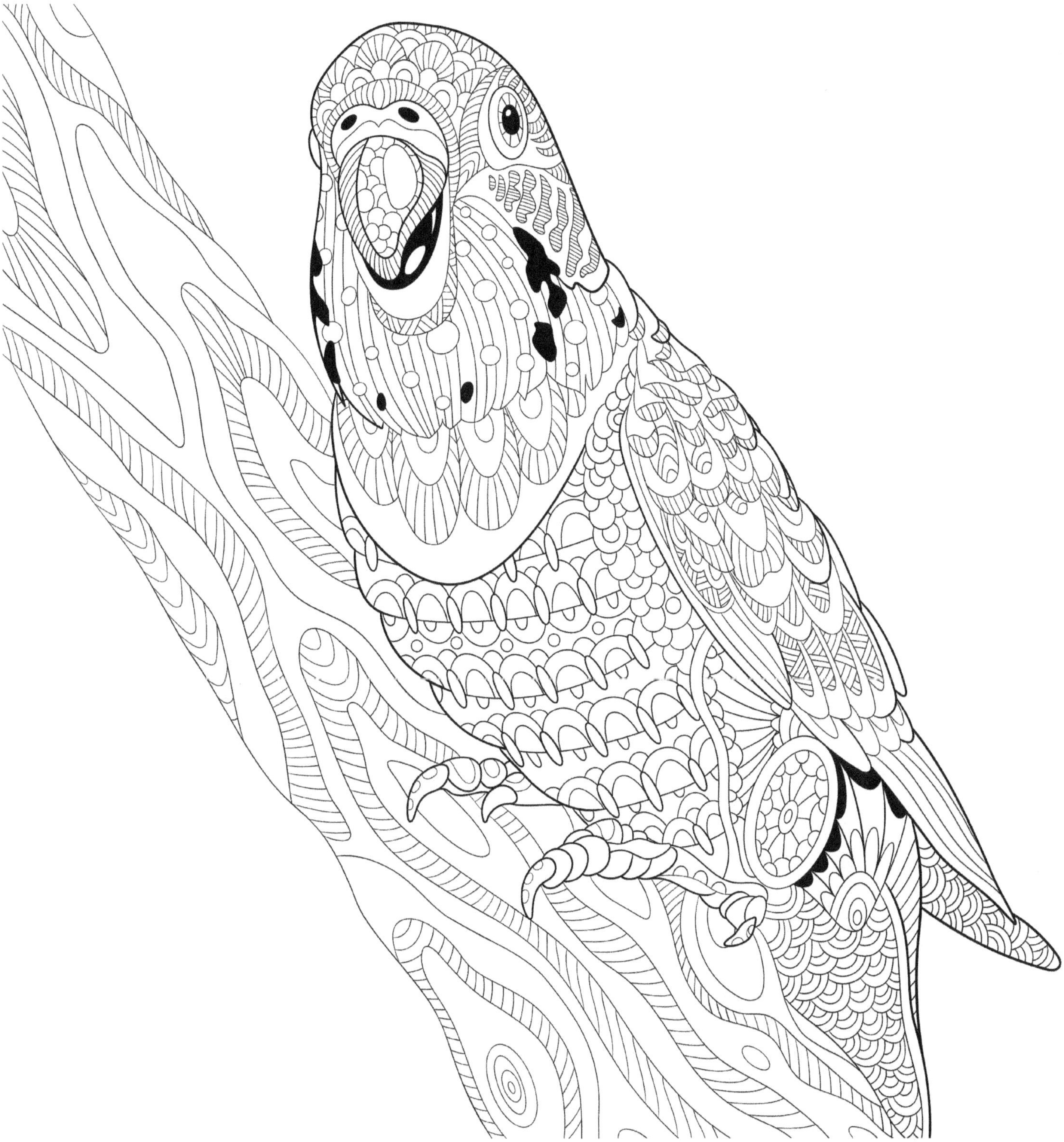

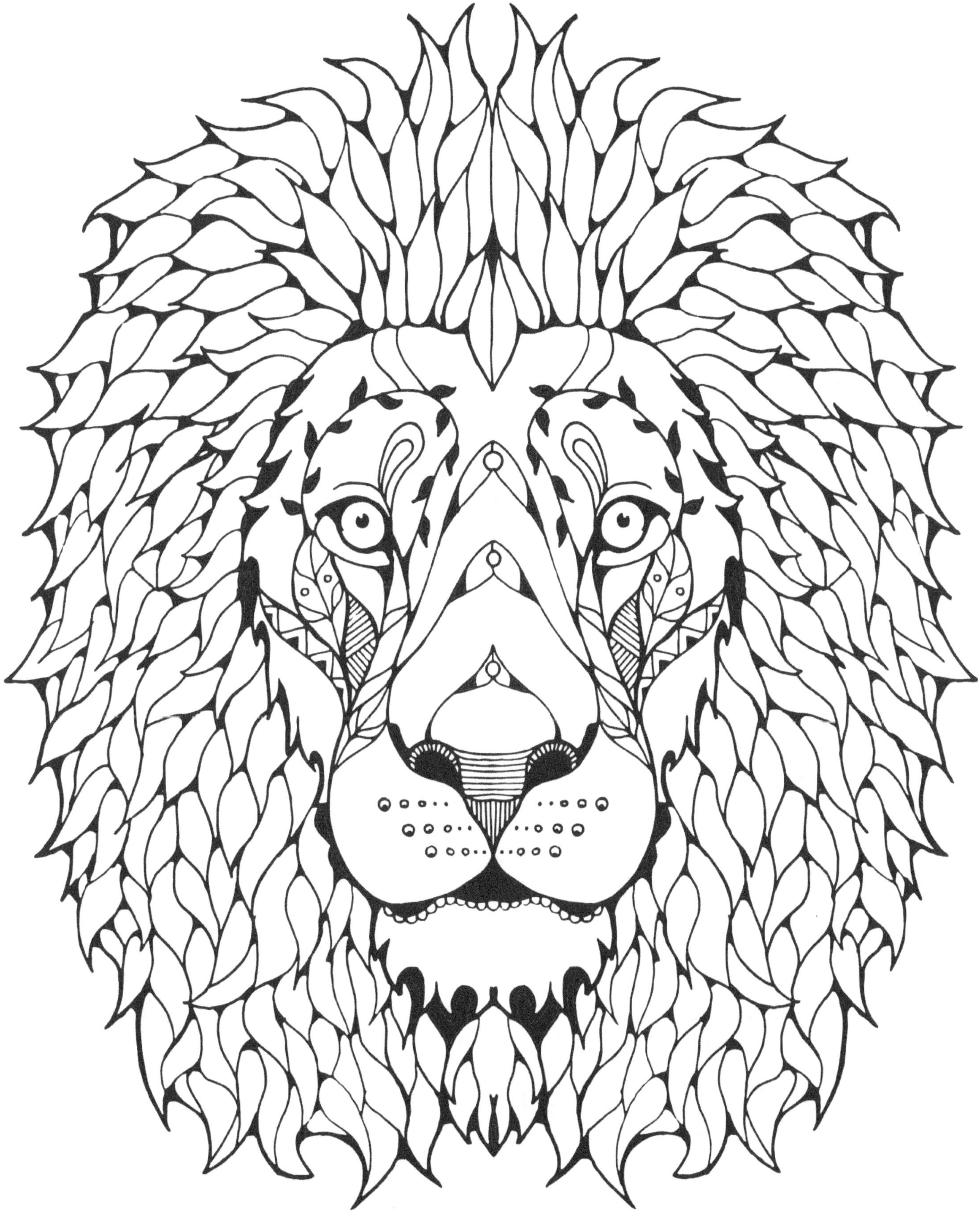

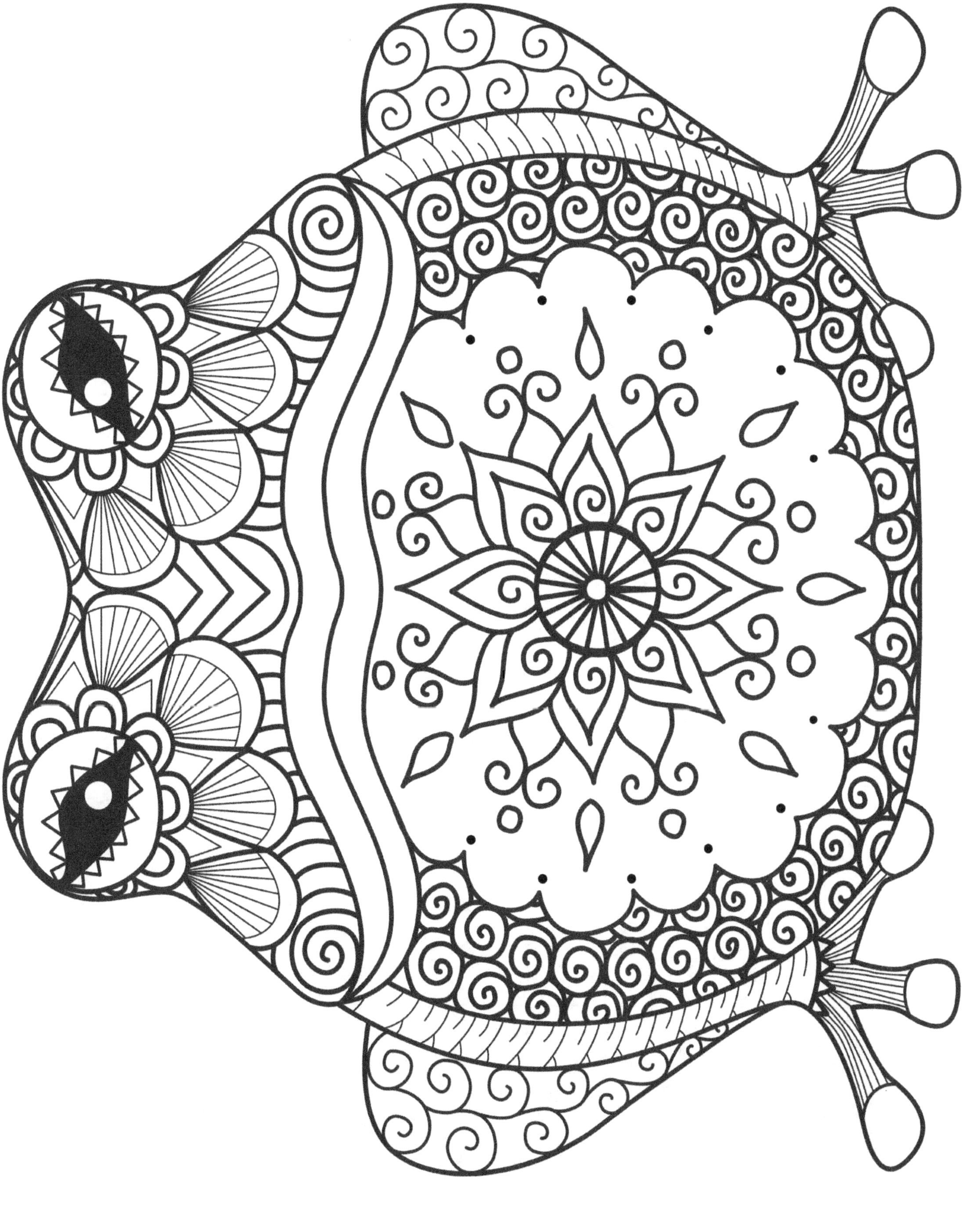

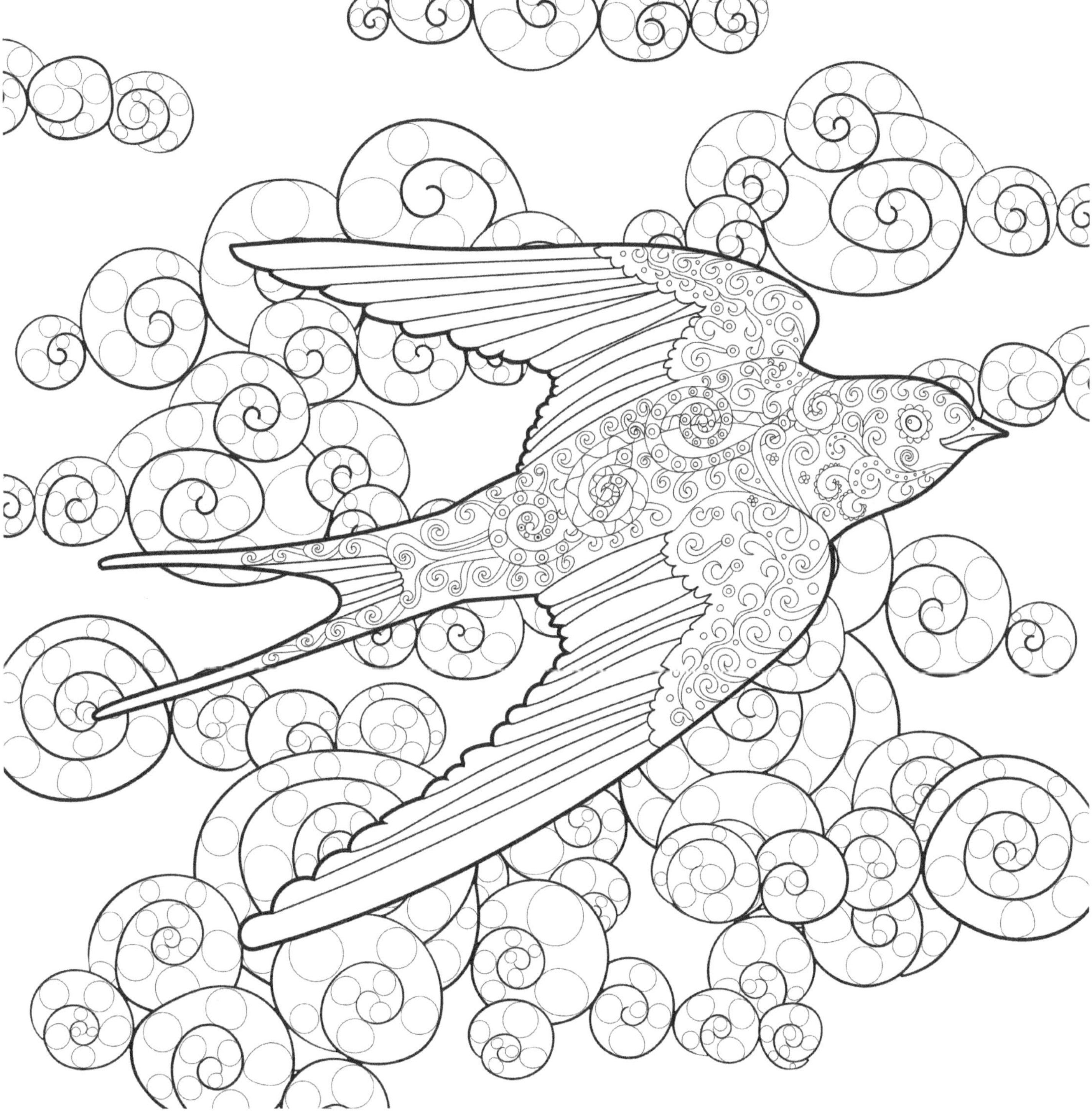

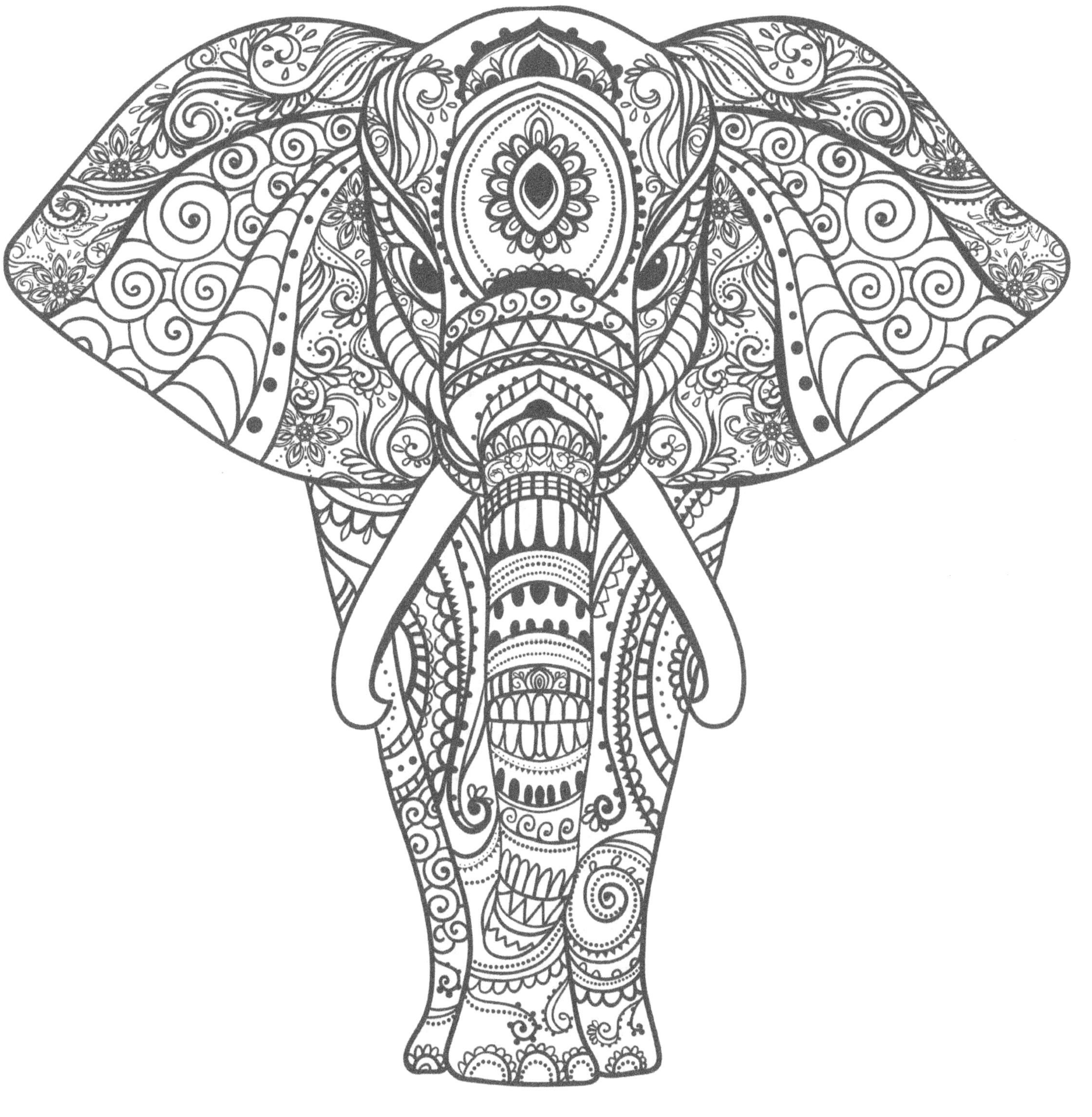

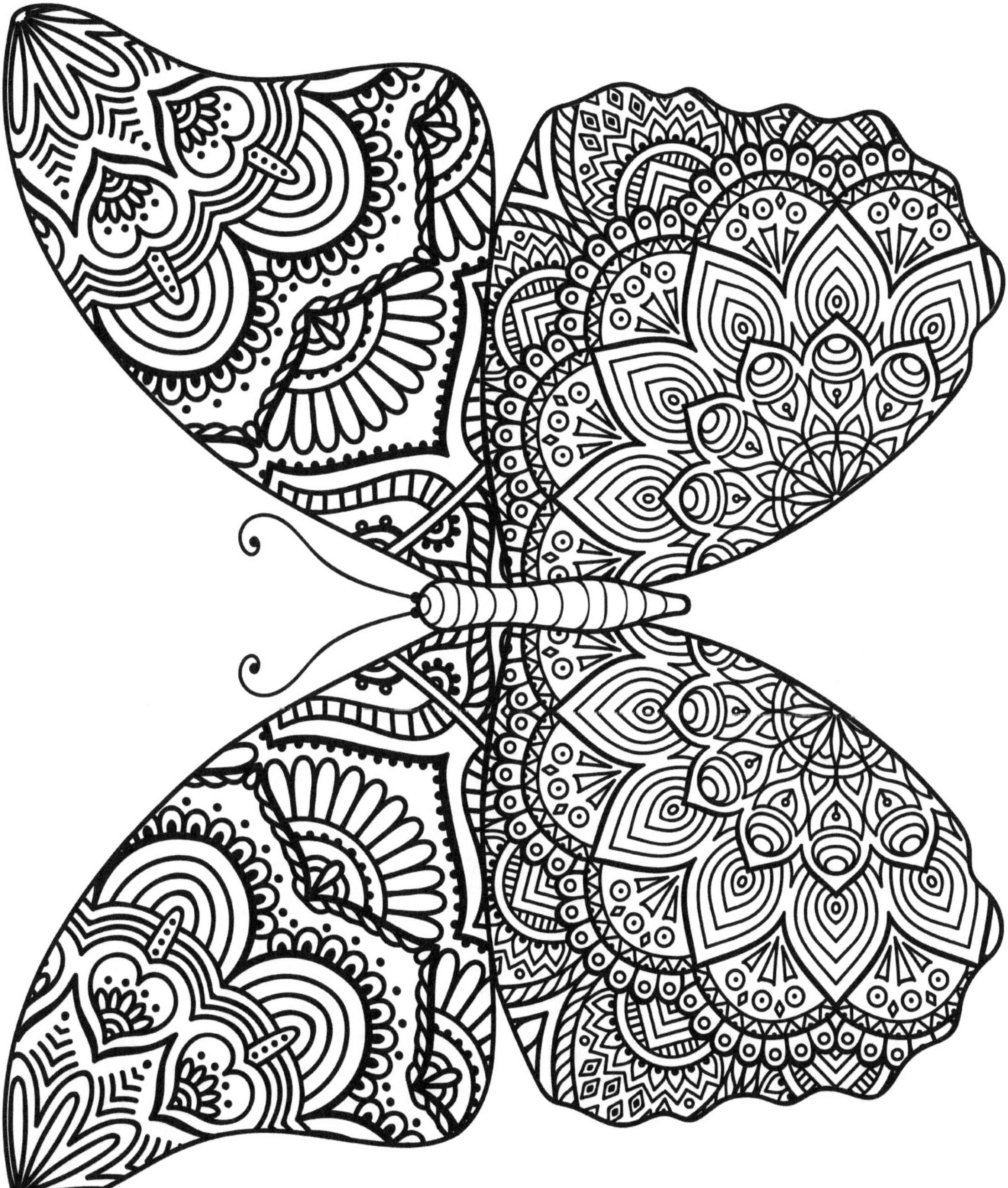

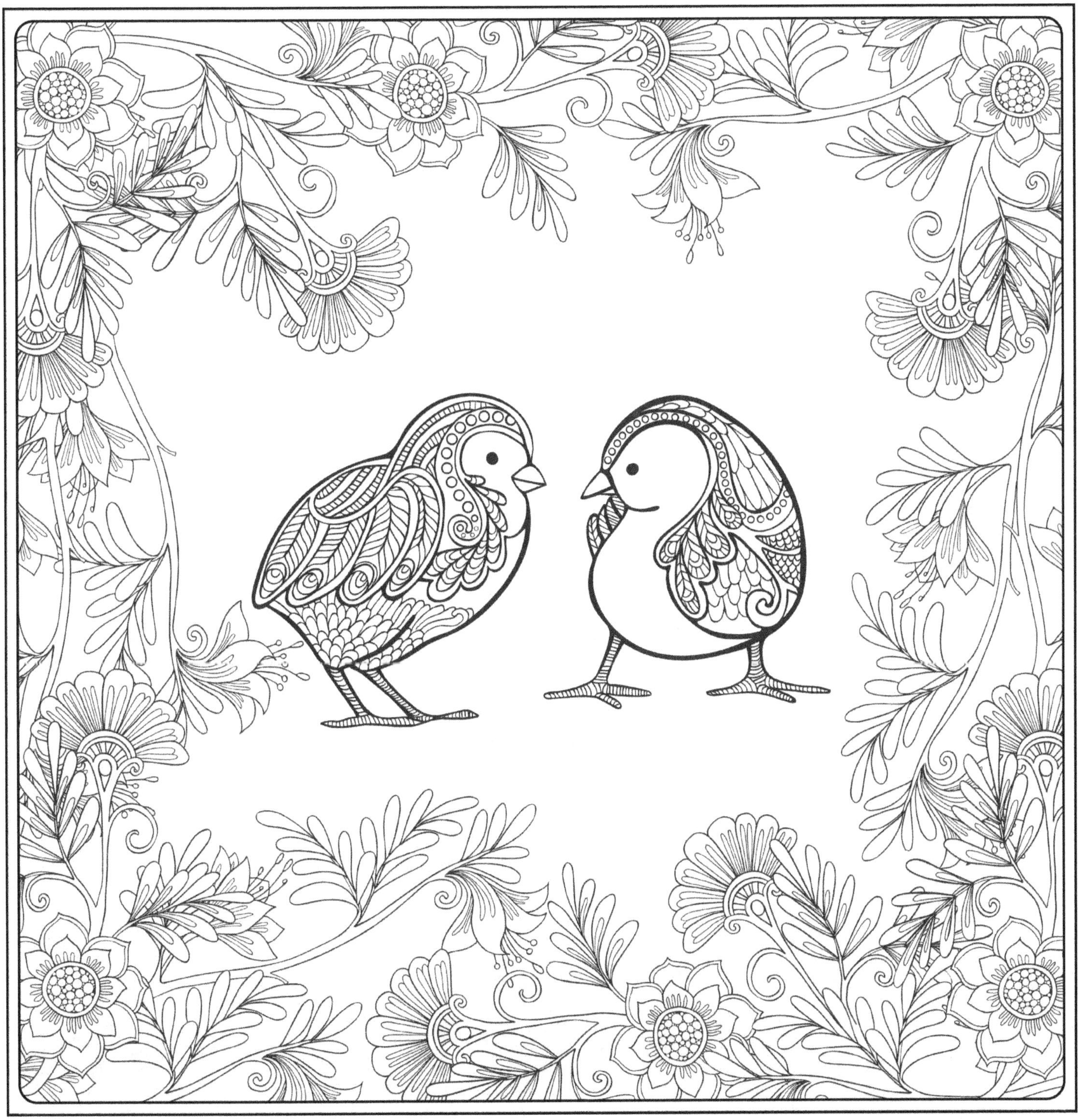

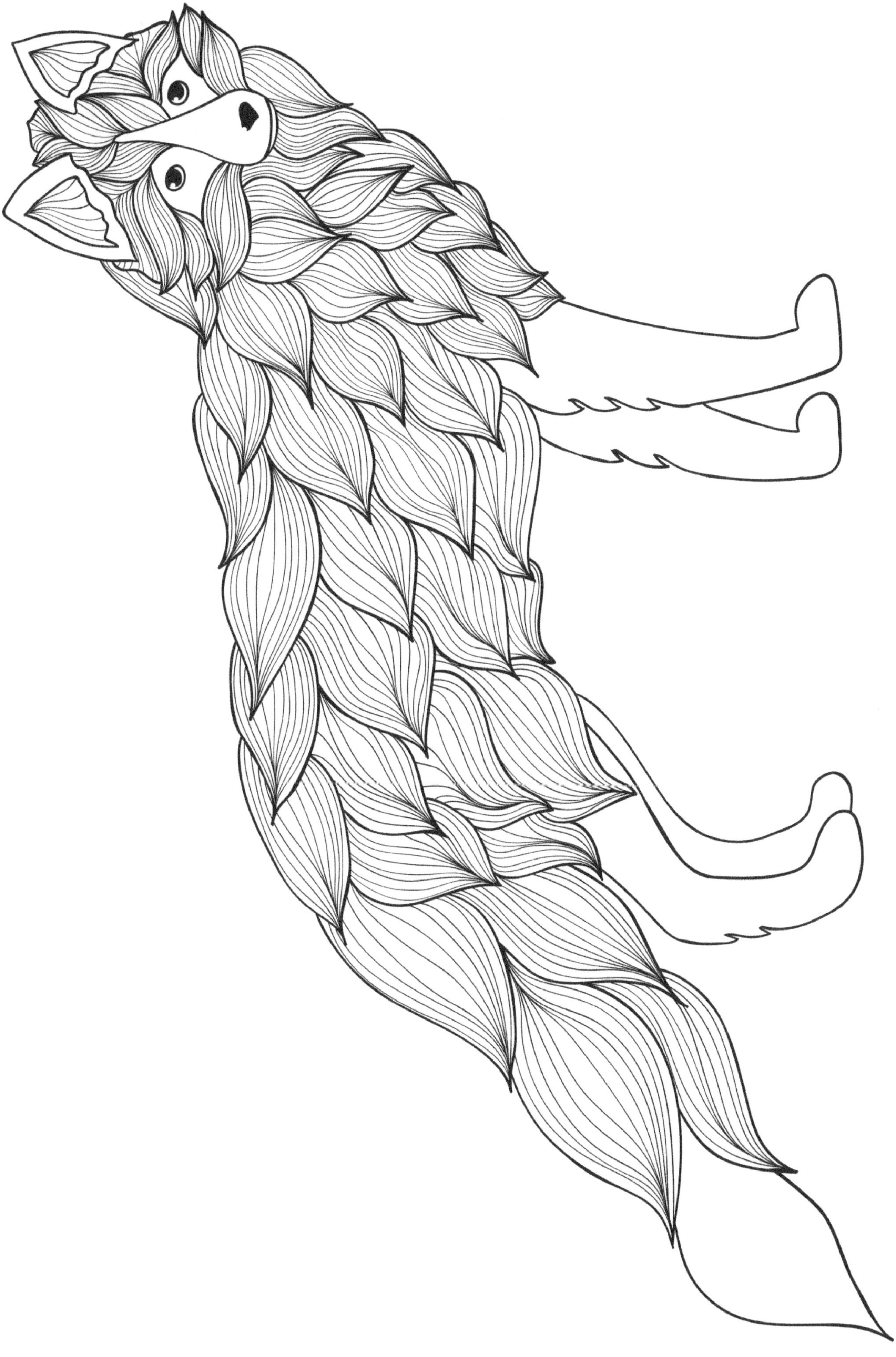

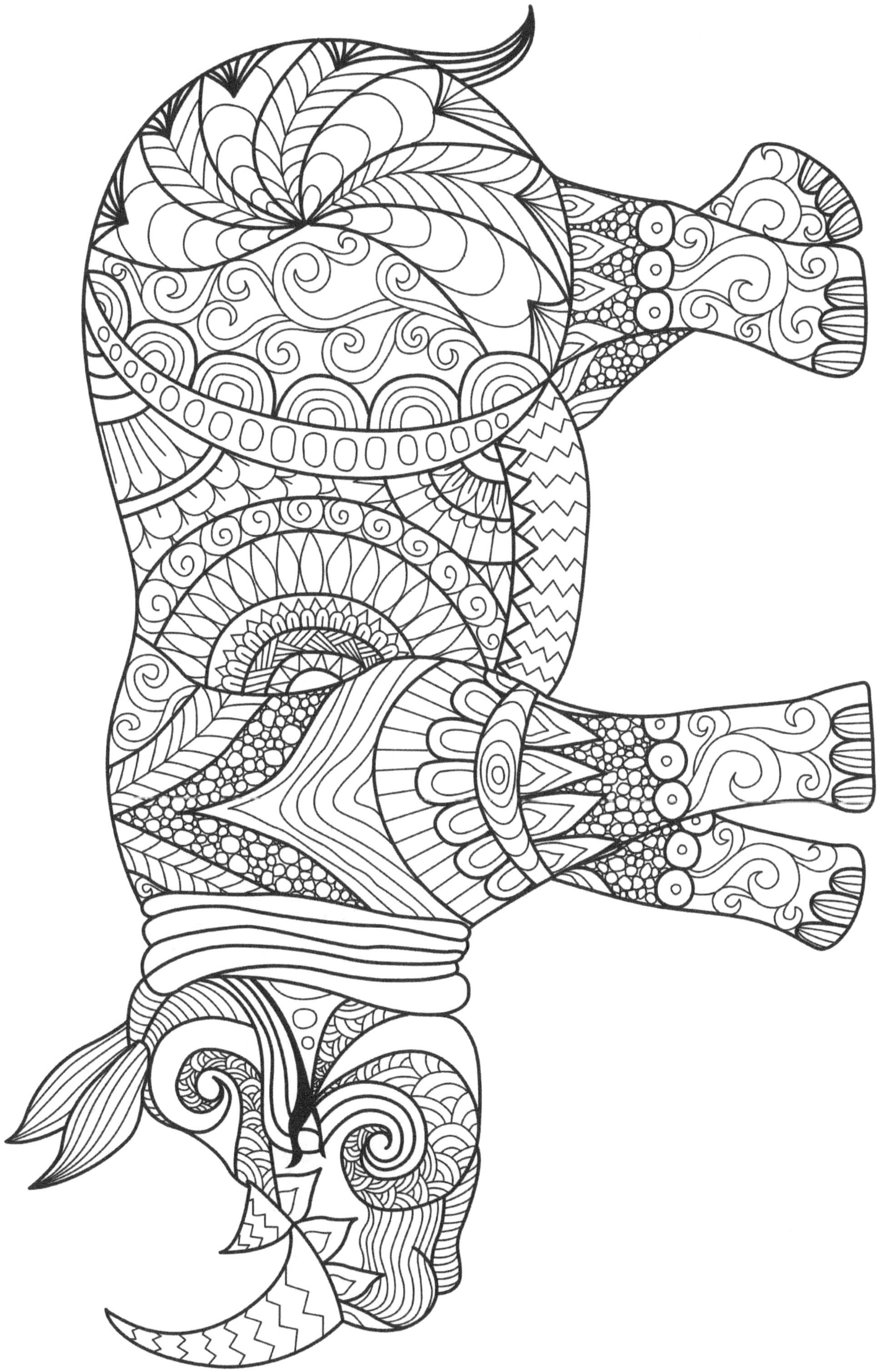

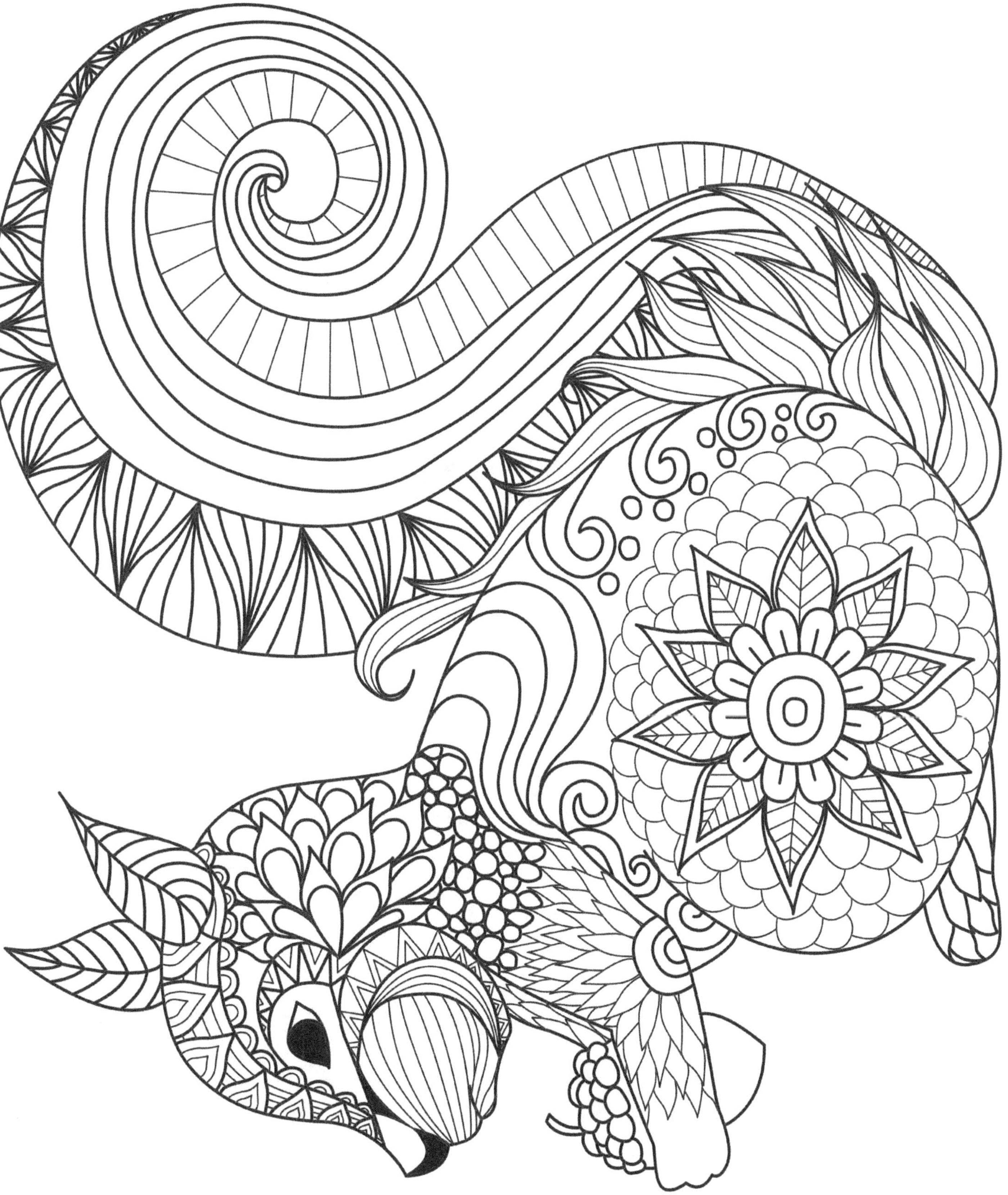

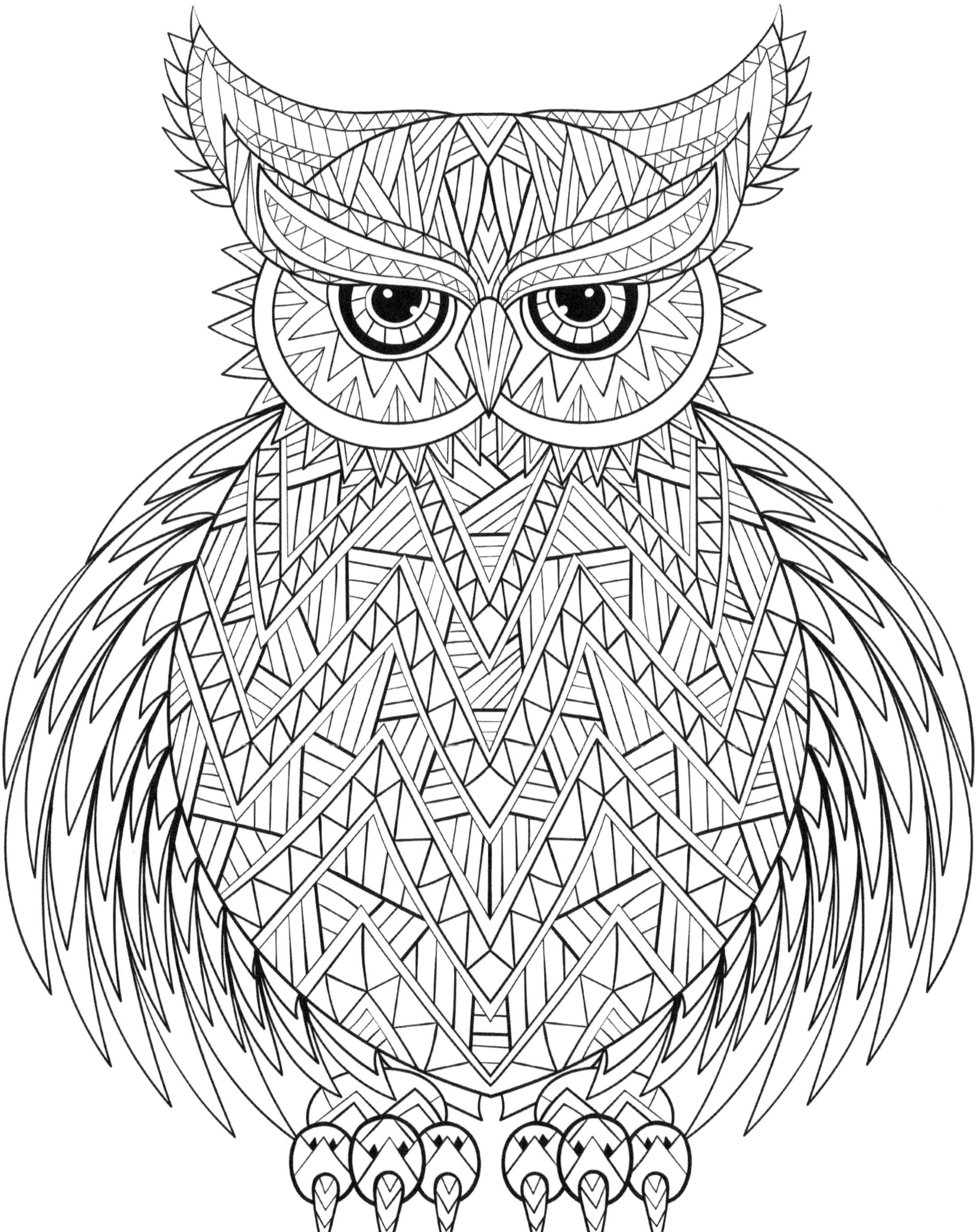

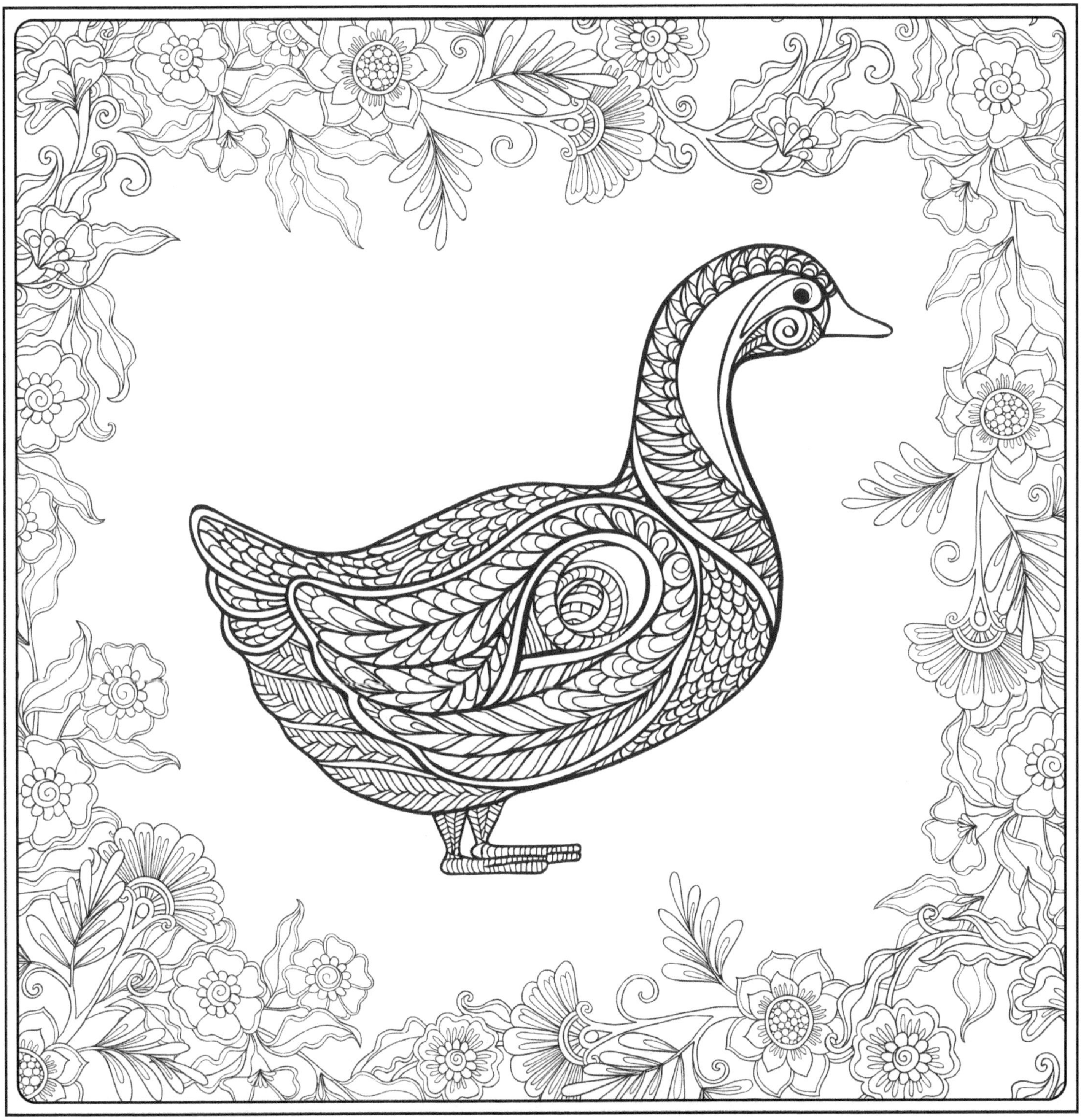

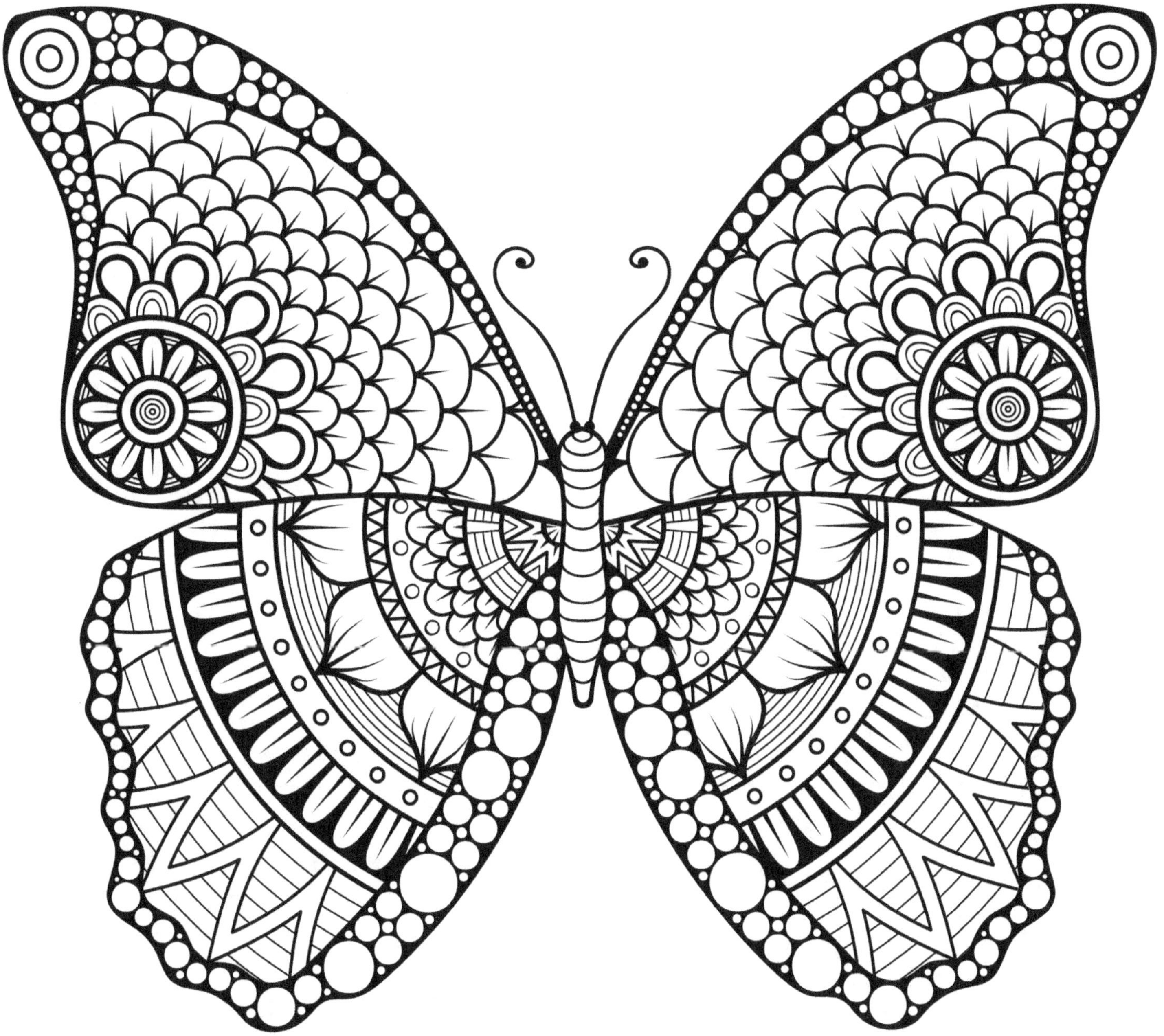

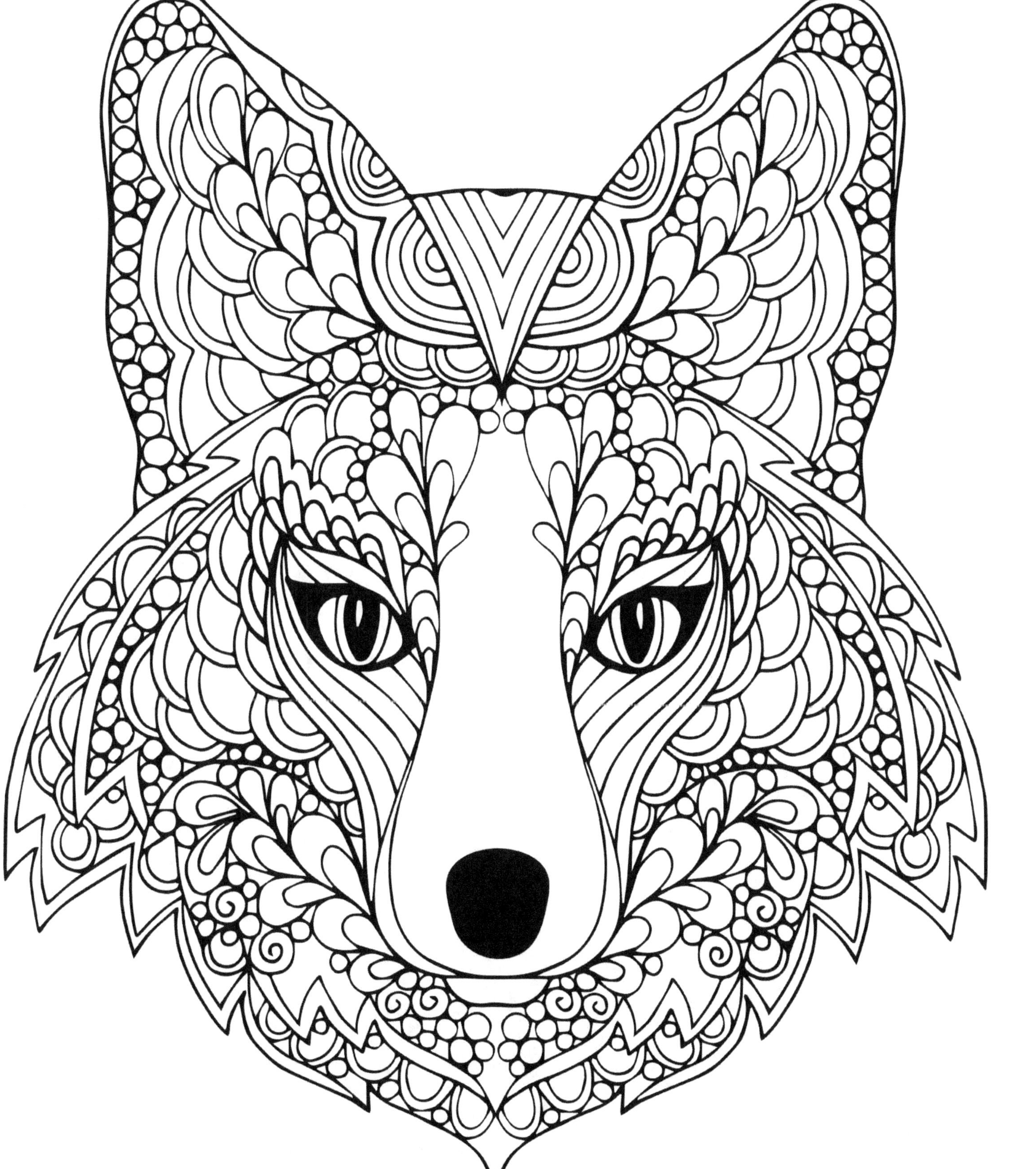

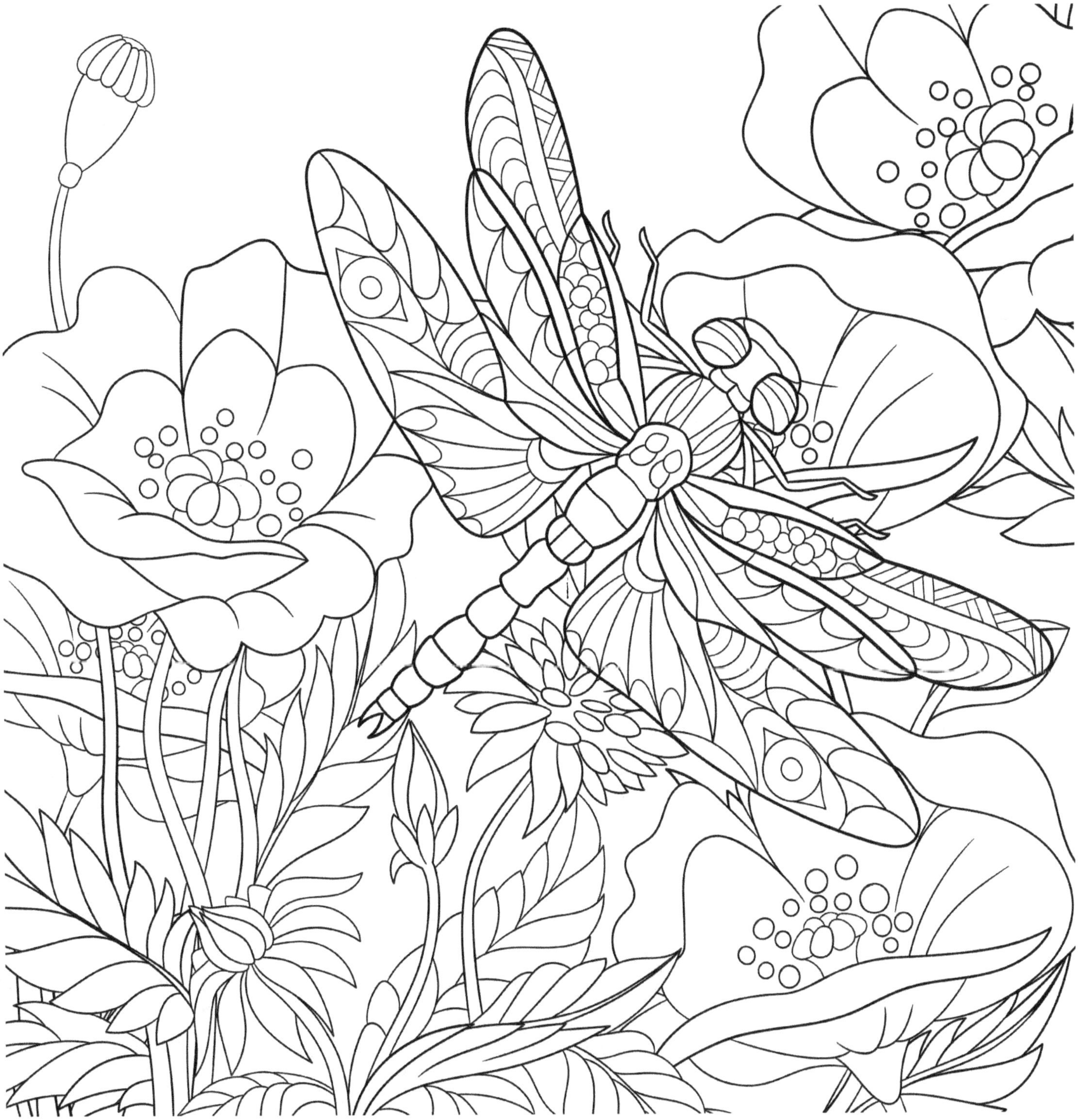

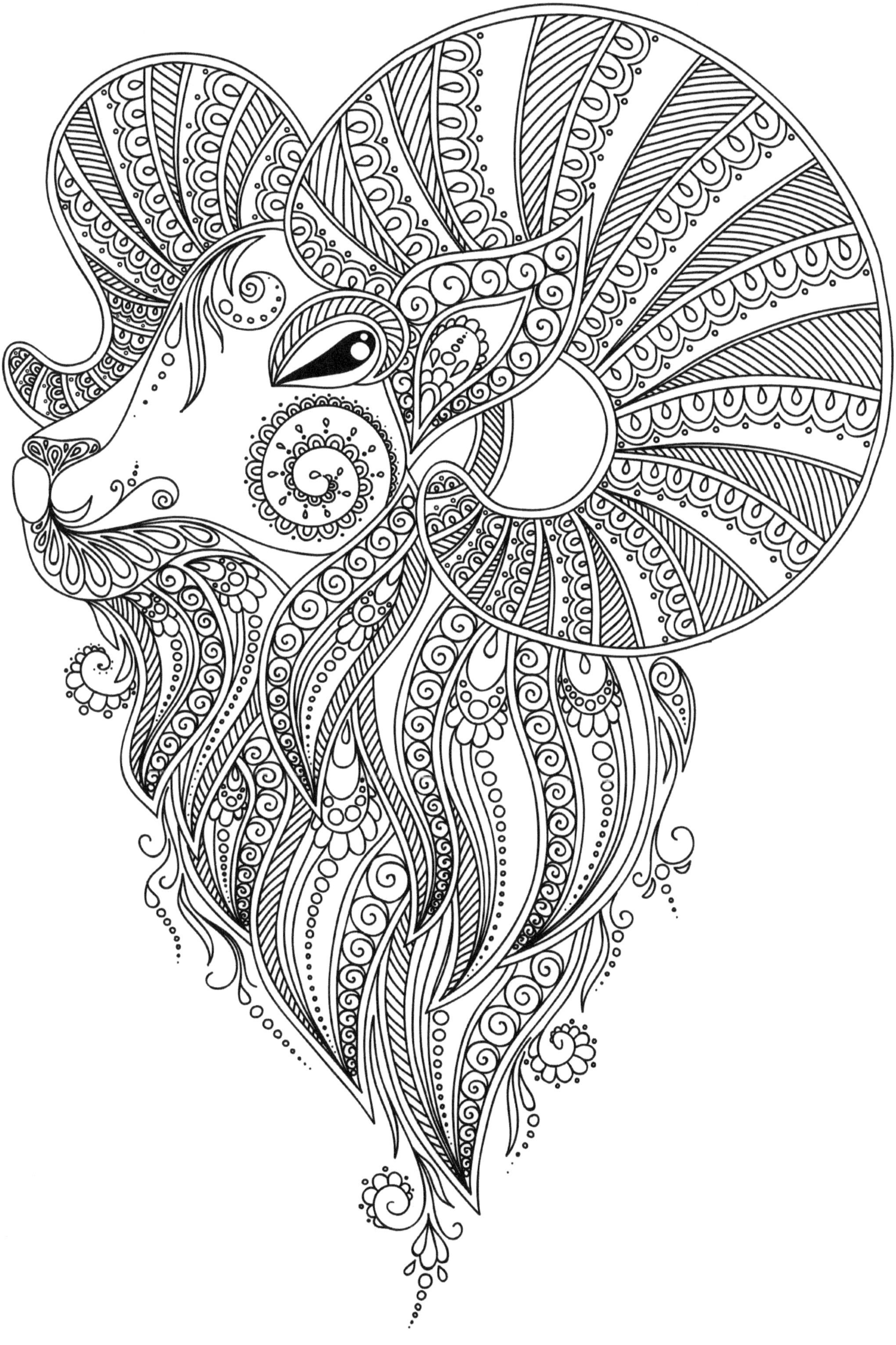

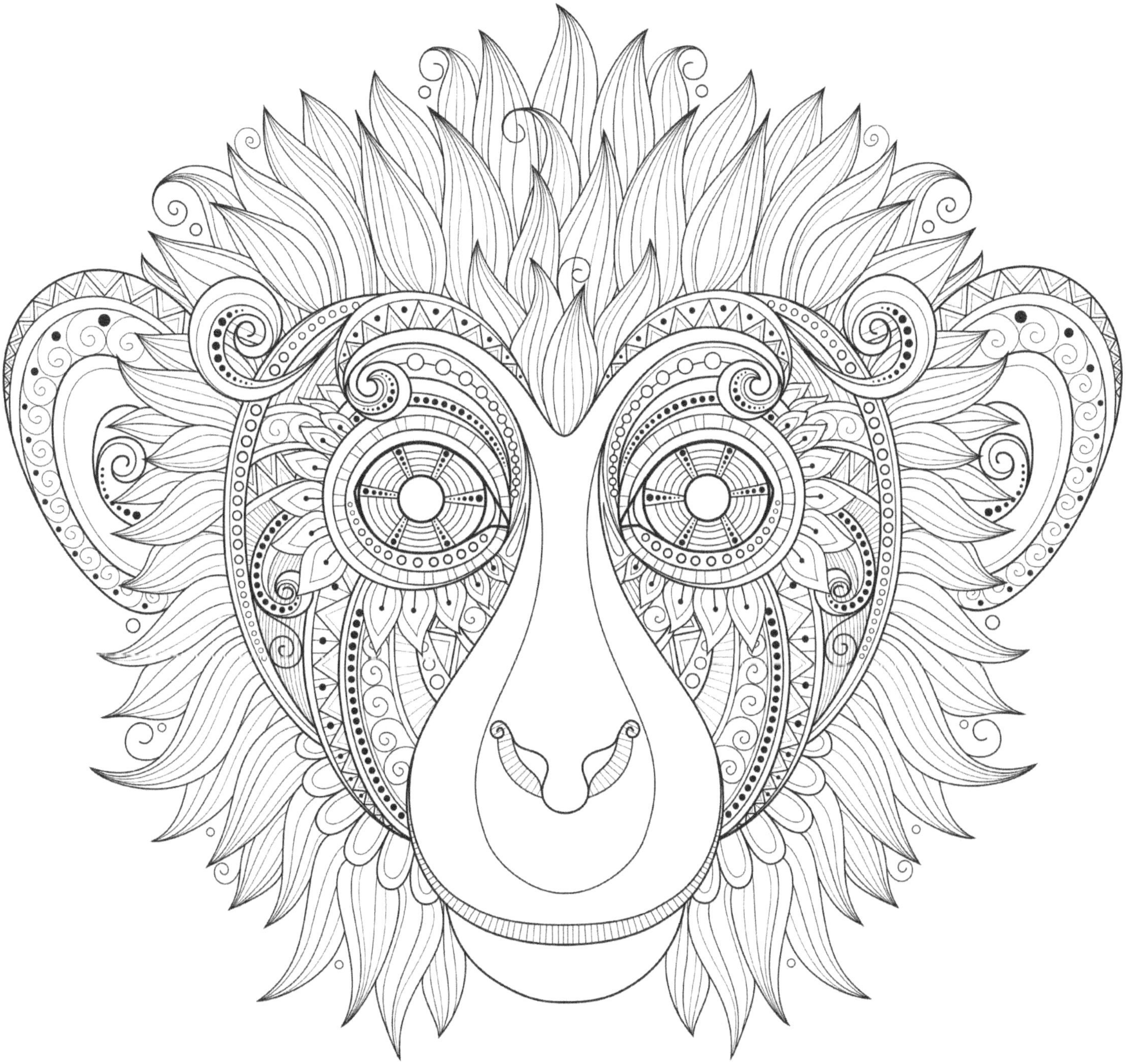

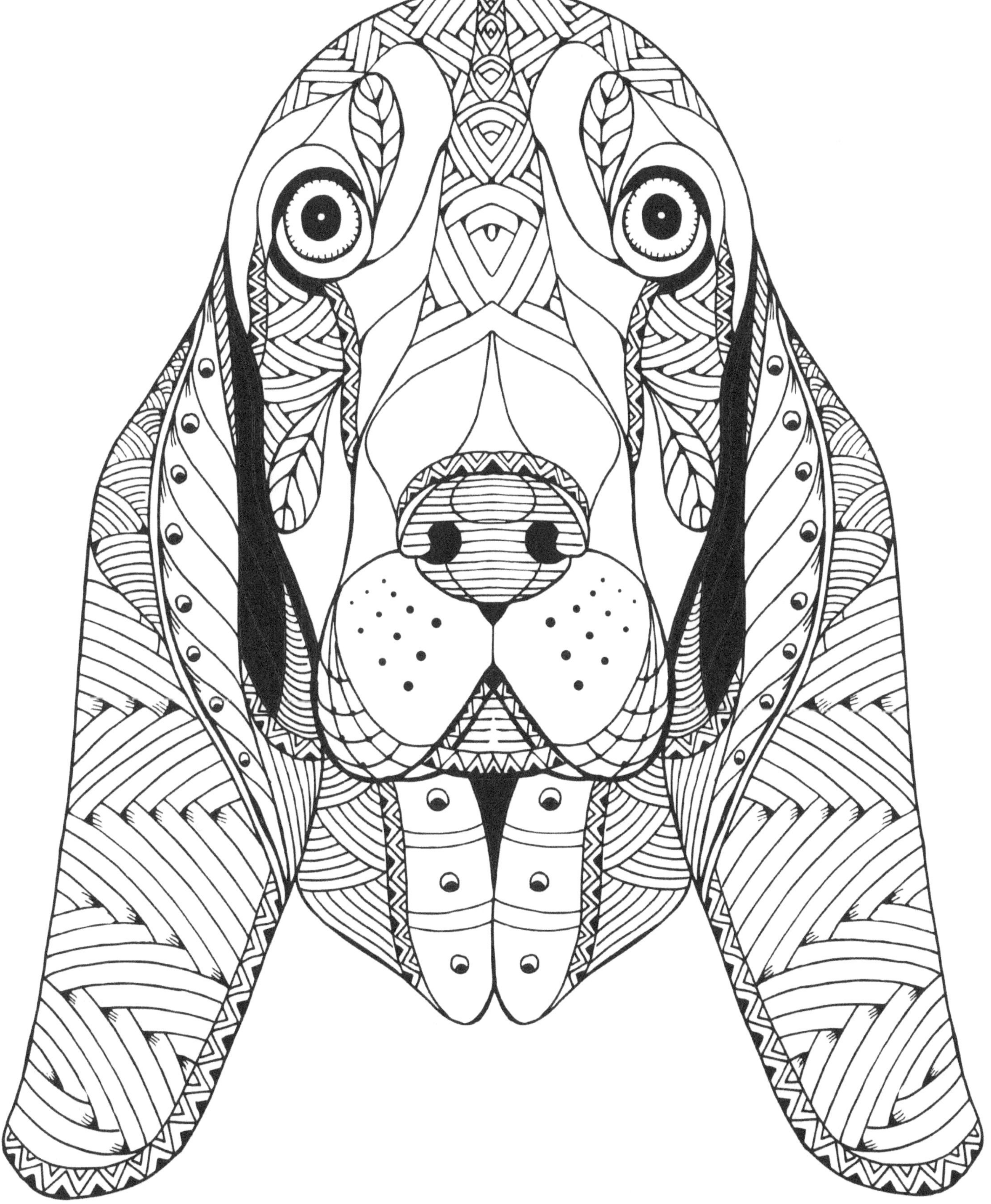

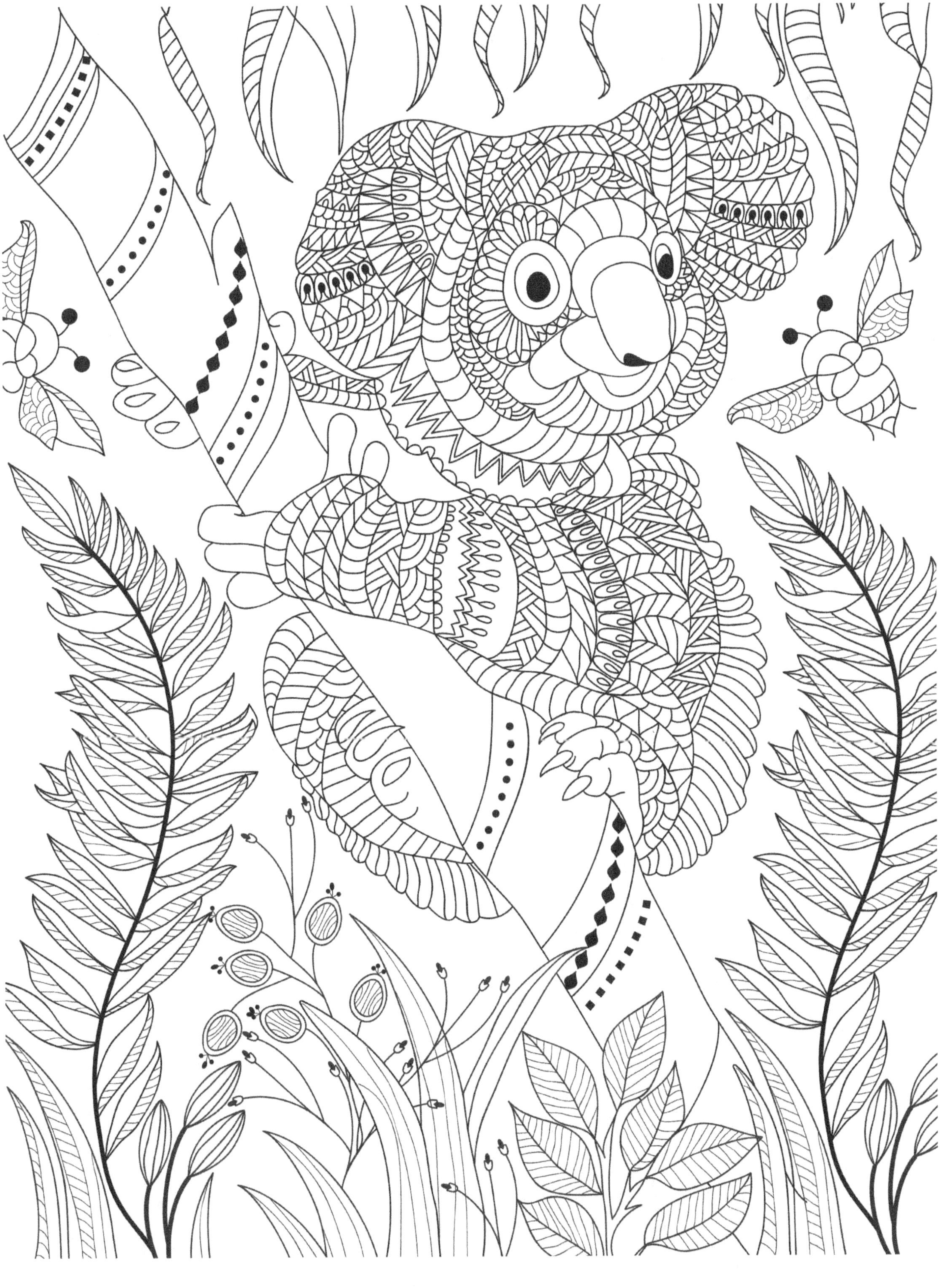

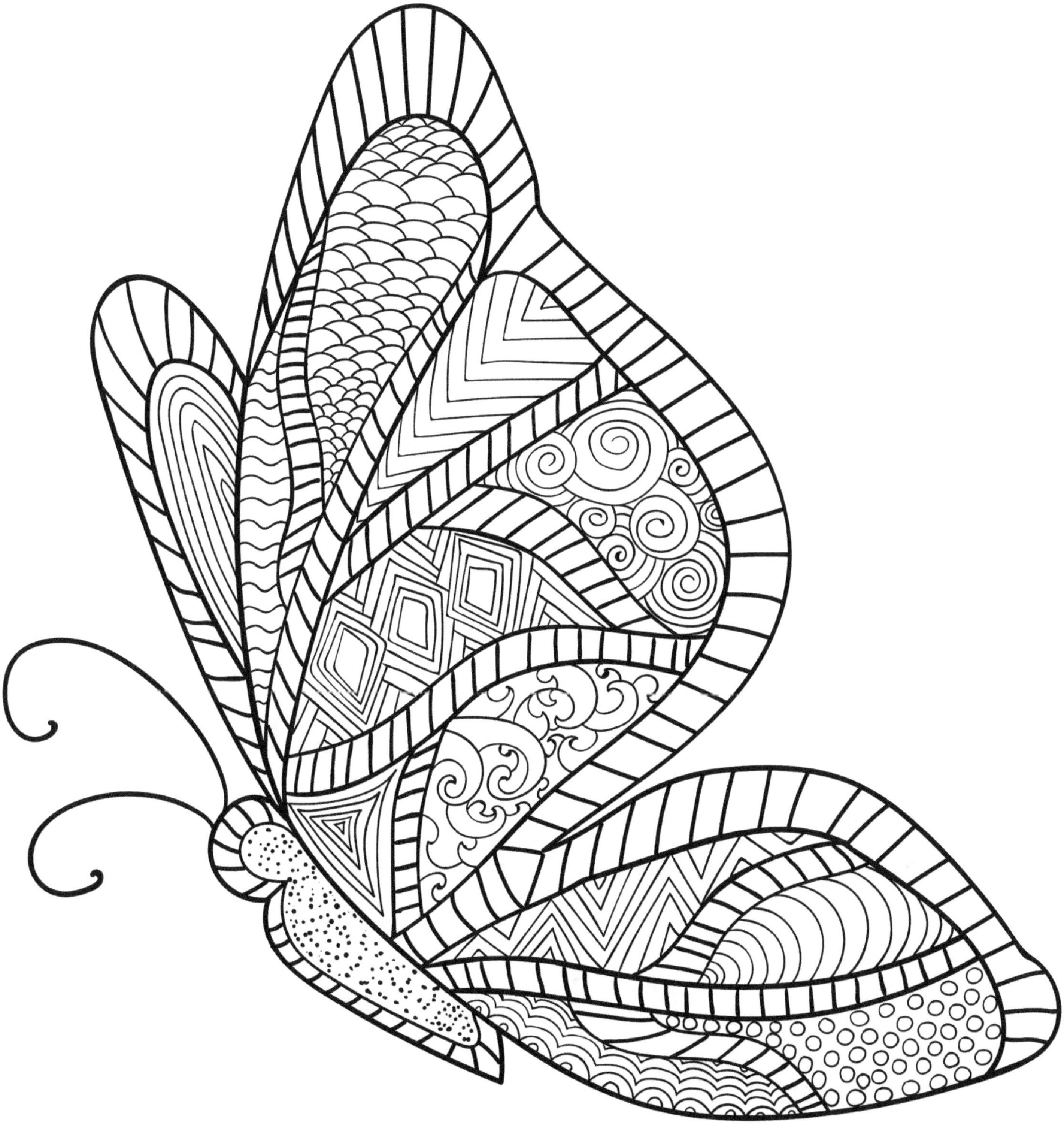

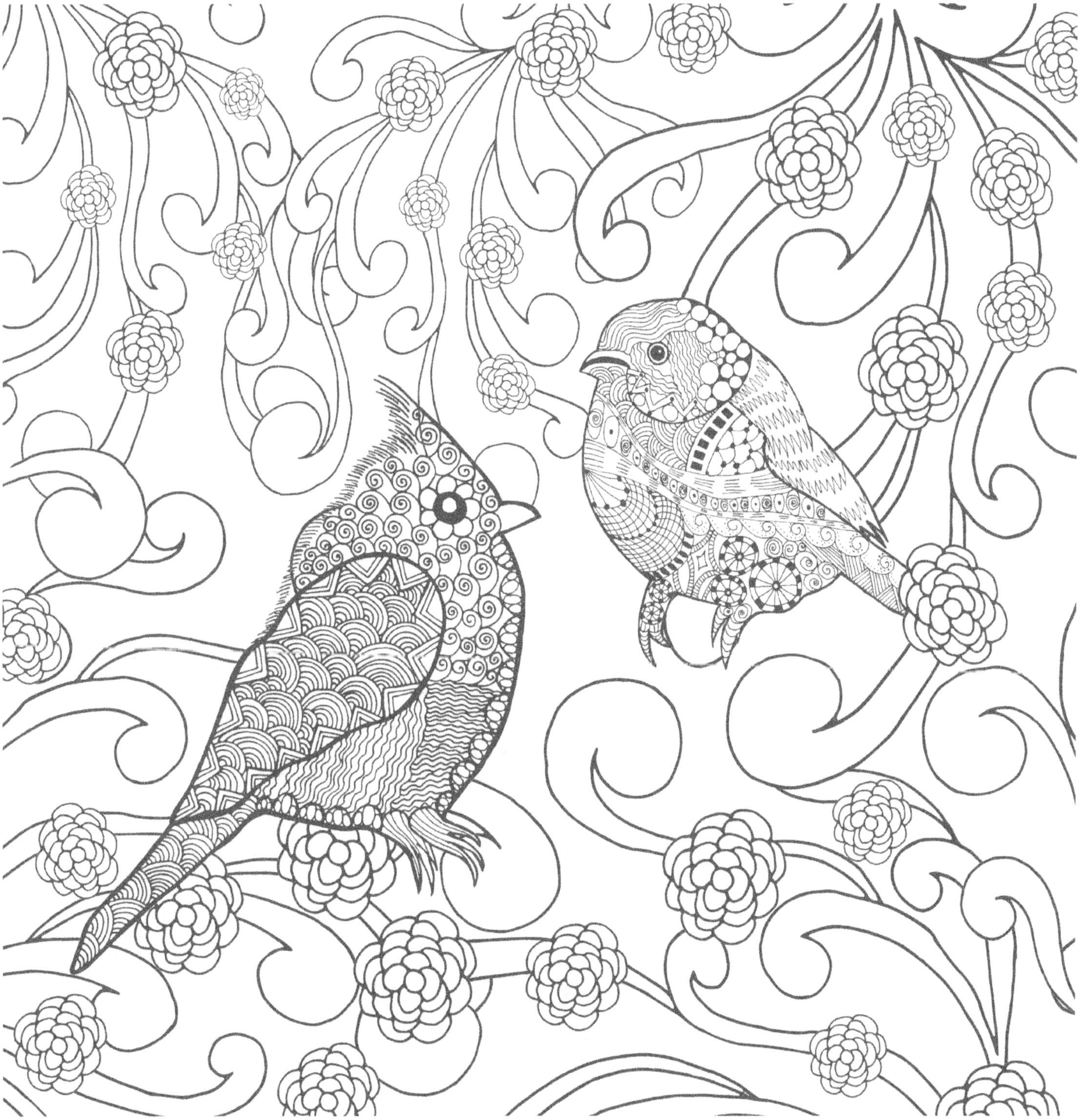

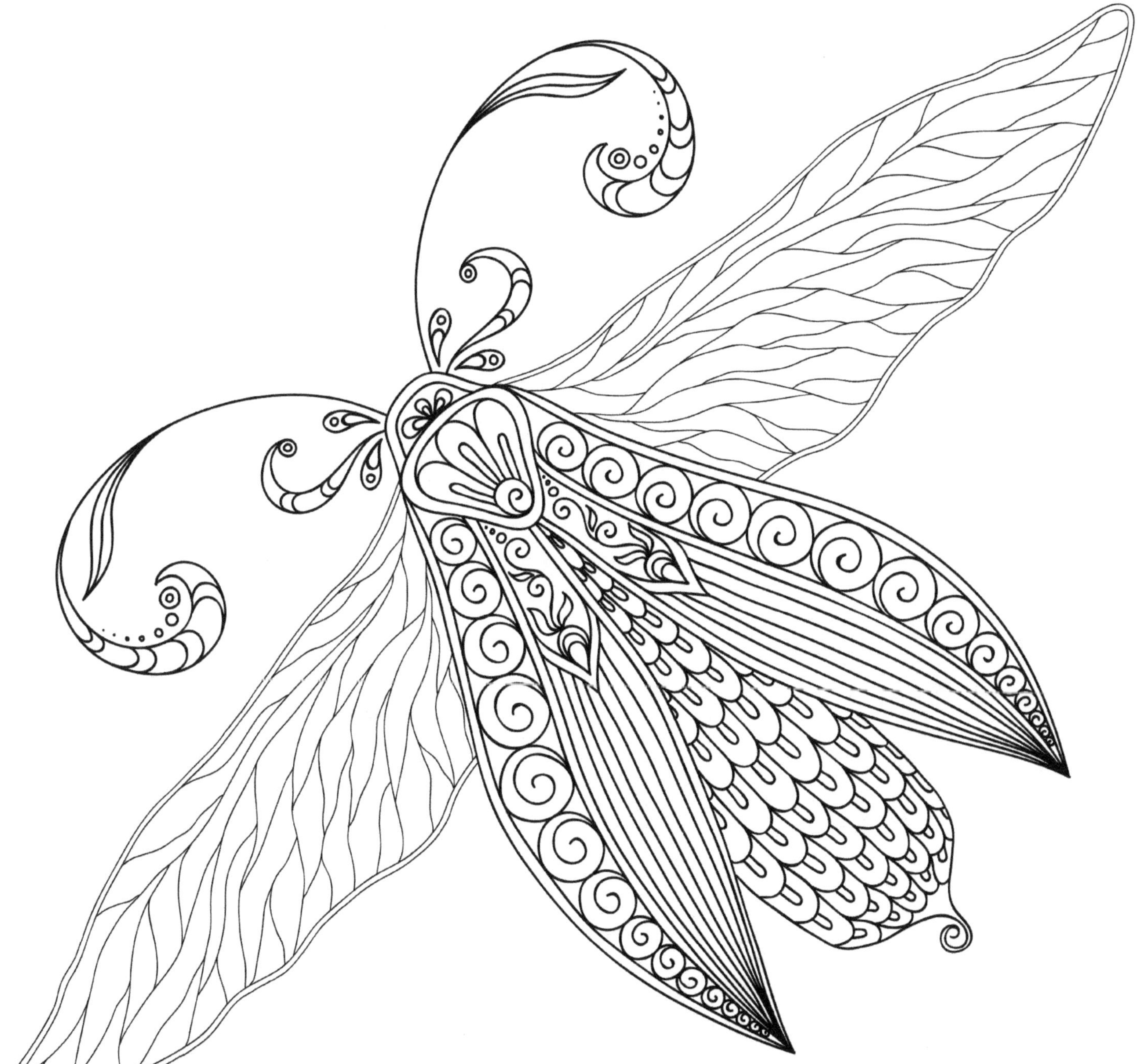

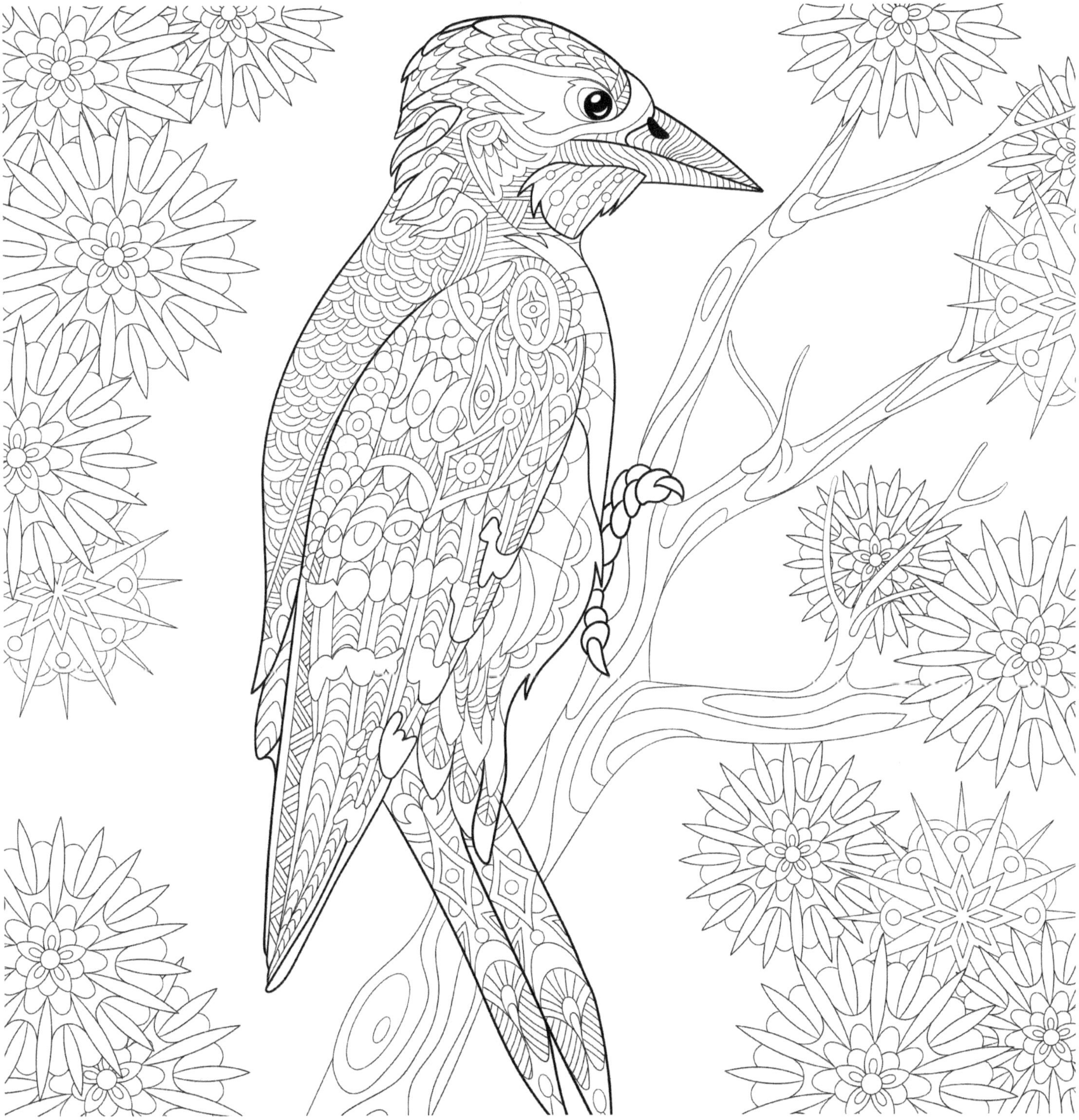

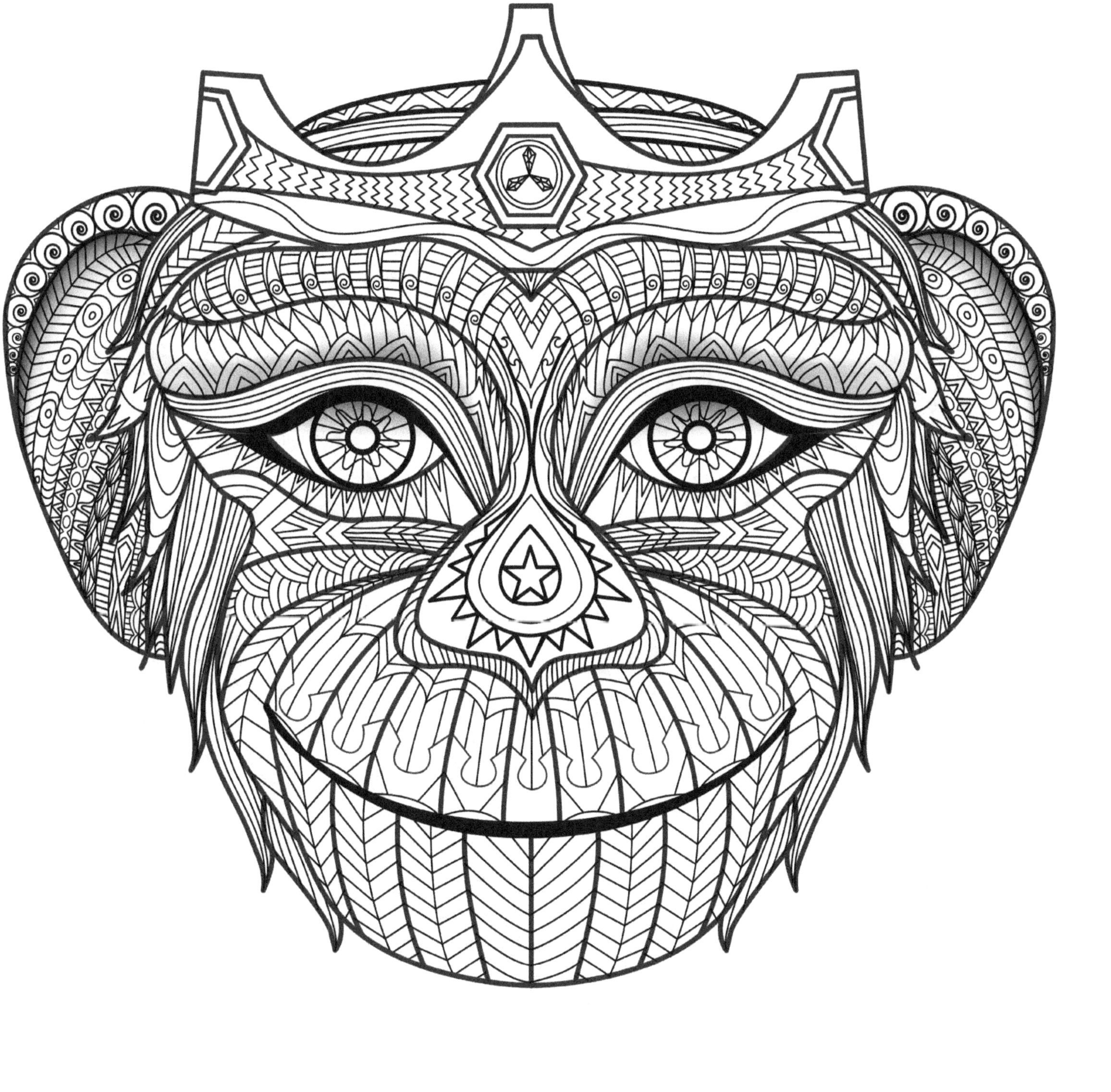

www.ingramcontent.com/pod-product-compliance
Lightning Source LLC
Chambersburg PA
CBHW080913170526
45158CB00008B/2096